The Basic Gourmet
Entertains

The Basic Gourmet
Entertains

Foolproof Recipes and Manageable Menus
for the Beginning Cook

✳

BY

Diane Morgan,
Dan Taggart, and Kathleen Taggart

PHOTOGRAPHY BY

Joyce Oudkerk Pool

CHRONICLE BOOKS

SAN FRANCISCO

✳ ✳ ✳

Library of Congress Cataloging-in-Publication Data
Morgan, Diane.
The basic gourmet entertains: foolproof recipes and manageable menus for the beginning
cook / by Diane Morgan, Dan Taggart, and Kathleen Taggart; photographs by Joyce Oudkerk Pool.
  p.   cm.
Includes index.
I S B N 0-8118-1428-9
1. Entertaining. 2. Cookery 3. Menus. I. Taggart, Dan. II. Taggart, Kathleen, 1951- . III. Title.
TX731. M587 1997
642′ .4–dc20   96-38846
CIP

Printed in Hong Kong

Food stylist: Susan Massey
Prop stylist: Carol Hacker
Book design and typesetting: Laurie Szujewska

The photographer would like to thank the following people for all their help, support
and generousity with props and locations: Gibson Scheid, American Rag
Maison, San Francisco, Cyclamen Studio, Berkeley, Annette Brands, Silvia Thornton

Distributed in Canada by Raincoast Books
8680 Cambie Street
Vancouver, British Columbia V6P 6M9

10 9 8 7 6 5 4 3 2 1

Chronicle Books
85 Second Street
San Francisco, California 94105

Web Site: www.chronbooks.com

✳

Acknowledgments

✳   ✳   ✳

As cooks and authors, we are keenly aware of the need for advice, counsel, and critique. No one who works with food can work in a vacuum. We are all the products of our background, culture, and history. Each of us comes to the table with a unique perspective. It was our goal throughout this project to listen and make use of many perspectives as we developed and tested recipes. We are sincerely grateful to all who participated.

Throughout our years of recipe writing, we have always felt it essential to have all recipes tested by an outside source. In this project, there is no one to whom we owe a greater debt of gratitude than David Berger, who, through his enthusiasm, became our chief tester. David literally gobbled up recipes as we gave them to him. His praise was genuine, and his criticisms, gentle and constructive. Many others tested for us as well and generously shared their thoughts. In no particular order they are Leslie Breaux, Anita Macdonald, Eric Watson, David Watson, Richard and Barbara LevKoy, Kathryn Taft Fovinci, Joan and Roger Cirillo, Sue and Tom Horstmann, David Hopkins and Rick Younge, Betty Shenberger, Lori Pellicano, and Marianne Barber. Teresa Schendel was also a wonderful tester, and her word processing skills were invaluable.

This project was unique in that as we talked about entertaining, we did it. Each menu was prepared as a unit and, as much as possible, was prepared for the number of guests suggested. We really had some fun times, and we wish to thank everyone who participated, because they all offered important ideas. We would party again anytime with Vance Selovar, Rody Ortega, Brenda Anderson, Priscilla and John Longfield, Cam and Tony Kimball, Marcy and Steve Taylor, Harriet and Peter Watson, Melinda and Jim Jackson, Stephanie Thieman, Bill Thieman, Christi Lee, Scott Hartman, Bob Lahatt, and Aaron and Susie Gross. Entertaining is always better in the company of Valerium di Pereira, Greg McCarty, Julie and Rocky Dixon, Geri Haber, Jeff Spurgeon, Tracy Roedl, Tom and Marcia Hamann, Pat and Scott Struckman, and Jane Burkholder. A very special thanks goes to Greg Morgan, whose superb palate remained well tuned even at the end of some phenomenally busy weeks. His active, behind-the-scenes counsel continues to be invaluable. Also, thanks go to the rest of the Morgan household, Eric and Molly, who taste, evaluate, and then give Mom the space to write.

We are also extremely grateful for the professional guidance and support we received from Elise and Arnold Goodman, Bill LeBlond, Leslie Jonath, Mary Ann Gilderbloom, and Judith Dunham. We owe a special debt of thanks to Jacqueline Killeen, who passed away after completing the editing of *The Basic Gourmet*. She taught us to speak with one voice, with brevity, and with thoughtfulness.

Contents

{ 2 }

BUFFETS

{ 1 }

ON-YOUR-FEET ENTERTAINING— STAND AND NIBBLE

{ 3 }

SIT-DOWN DINNERS

Introduction

THIS BOOK IS ABOUT having fun while entertaining guests in your home.

As a beginning cook, you have tried various recipes, had some successes, built some confidence, and bingo! now you want to share your exploits with friends, family, and colleagues. Now the challenge begins–it's called entertaining.

What the confident new cook typically lacks is a road map, or a set of directions, that will take the beginner from mastering individual recipes to putting a meal or party together for invited guests. *The Basic Gourmet Entertains* provides you with that road map.

Entertaining is the joy of putting all of your culinary and social talents together to produce a meal for others. Being a good host can be immensely satisfying. Good food and drink have a special effect on people. Many of our best and most lasting friendships have grown out of evenings spent around a table in someone's home.

Hosting an event, no matter what size, takes equal parts of menu planning, household organization, cooking skill, and attention to guests. This book is intended to make you, the host, feel relaxed, not intimidated. Our menus blend international cuisines, but we call for ingredients readily available in most supermarkets. We offer tips on advance planning, pre-party organization, timing, and equipment and serving pieces you will need, as well as suggestions for handling all those last-minute details.

Cooks who serve simple menus well are more likely to be remembered as good hosts than cooks who try to impress with fancy foods beyond their experience. Simply put, a perfect hamburger served by an attentive host who keeps wine (or maybe lemonade) glasses full can be great entertaining. Getting fancy beyond your level of comfort is just a recipe for stress, not fun.

Every experienced cook, though maybe not wanting to admit it, has had entertaining disasters. The dinner that was supposed to be served at 7 P.M. but wasn't ready until 9 P.M. The pork roast that was overcooked, and, oops, the small kitchen fire that resulted from failing to check the water level in the steamer. Well, we have all been there, done that, and now we know! Just remember, good hosts don't take themselves too seriously and they have a sense of humor about kitchen mishaps. Best of all, we can teach you how to avoid the pitfalls and actually have fun while you entertain others.

So, let the parties begin!

About Entertaining at Home

✳   ✳   ✳

Do you like to eat well? Do you enjoy the company of other people? If you answered yes to both questions, you already have the makings of a good host!

There is real joy in serving food you have made to guests you have invited into your home. While it is work–no doubt about that–the rewards are manifest. Personal bonds are closest among those who have opened their homes to friends (new or old) and those who have enjoyed the host's personal hospitality. Entertaining in one's home is both a job and an honor; it is work and it ought to be fun. It takes planning ahead and attention to guests' needs. It inevitably involves after-hours cleanup. But there is no feeling like the one that arises when a departing guest looks you in the eye and says, "What a great evening! Thanks for including me."

When the doorbell rings, the fun starts. That's the way it should be, and that's the way it *will* be– if you give a little thought to your guests' needs before they arrive. Good hosting can be elevated to an art form, but it starts with simple planning. That is one of the things this book is about.

Entertaining need not bankrupt the host. Complicated foods, expensive wine labels, and fancy decorations don't guarantee a successful party. Simple, straightforward meals served with care are more likely to be appreciated than haphazardly prepared, expensive menus. A whole roast tenderloin of beef is a fabulous entrée (which you'll find in this book), but so is a sautéed breast of chicken. A hundred-dollar spray of flowers will undoubtedly draw attention, but a single hand-cut tulip in an old glass milk jar is just as elegant in its own way. Serving inexpensive but well-made wine whose taste you like will allow you to be generous with guests, whereas choosing a snobby label might lead to parsimonious pouring. Guests instinctively know when you are giving of yourself–your time, your cooking ability–rather than throwing money at a party.

Getting organized is the first step if you want to have fun entertaining. Even a little dinner for four requires thought about menu, cooking timing, serving pieces, and so on. Needless to say, a buffet for fifty is a bit more demanding. We suggest you consider the following advice.

- Be flexible about menus, including ours. Be sure to review our Mixed-Up Menus (page 158) for ideas on combining recipes from this book in different ways.

- Do as much advance cooking preparation as possible. Our menus have very clear strategies for what we think can be done ahead. Don't save all the cooking for the last minute–it is a great way to appear frazzled to your guests and leave you regretting the whole affair. Many foods freeze quite well if properly wrapped, and many dishes survive happily in the refrigerator for several days before your event.

- Lay out all serving pieces required by the menu so there are no last-minute surprises. Remember to allow small plates or bowls at buffets for discarded toothpicks, chicken or rib bones, or olive pits. Use your imagination in selecting serving pieces–soup tastes just as good served from a nice-looking saucepan as it does from a fancy soup tureen. Presentation may be half the art of good living, but by all means don't cancel the party for lack of impressive china!

- Arrange the party space well before guests arrive. Flowers are a terrific way to dress up a room. So are candles–unscented if you want your food to be enjoyed to its fullest. Lighting should be appropriate for the time of day, neither so dark guests can't see their plates nor so bright that 8 P.M. seems like noon.

- Buy amounts needed for the event or have a plan for using leftovers. Try to buy wine at a case discount price. Sometimes you must buy twelve bottles of the same wine, or sometimes an assortment of twelve bottles. Many supermarkets and most specialty-wine merchants offer some kind of case discount. Pick wines you like and can afford, and would like multiple bottles of.

- Give accurate and complete event information, whether verbal or written. Guests ought to know when, where (include a map if necessary), style of dress, and what kind of eating to expect ("cocktails and light hors d'oeuvres," "dinner," "buffet supper"). If your party is from 3 P.M. to 6 P.M. on a Sunday afternoon, most people will expect nibbles, not dinner. If it is from 6 P.M. to 9 P.M. and it is *not* dinner, your guests have a need to know what to expect, so they can make dinner plans and not be tempted to eat you out of house and home unexpectedly!

- Ask for an RSVP on your written invitation if you need to know how many people *will* attend (for a sit-down dinner, for example). The RSVP indicates that you would like the courtesy of a response one way or another. If you need a general idea of the crowd size (for a Sunday-afternoon open house, say) then "Regrets Only" is a way to ask for a response if a guest *cannot* attend.

Entertaining is all about making guests feel at home in your home. Plan for nonalcoholic drink requests. Have available fruit spritzers (page 17) or plain seltzer water with lemon or lime—something refreshing and not too sweet to go with food. Be accommodating to vegetarian requests if you get them. Meatless dishes are not hard to arrange if a guest gives you a little notice, which he or she ought to do at the time of accepting your invitation. If a guest arrives and announces vegetarian leanings at the last minute, smile politely and offer to help in whatever way you can. Often the entrée plate (minus the meat, fowl, or fish) can be augmented by vegetables or fruit already on hand.

Never skimp on food quality. Use the ingredients called for in the recipe. Never substitute low-fat or nonfat ingredients unless you have previously tested the dish and are pleased with the results. Your guests deserve better than a last-minute experiment or guilt trip. If low-fat or low-calorie needs dictate, you should plan the menu accordingly, not cheat on the recipe ingredients.

Most of all, enjoy the company of your guests! This will be possible because you have planned ahead and not trapped yourself into doing too many last-minute tasks. Inviting friends to join you for dinner, or brunch, or buffet supper, will likely become a lifelong habit. Your guests are your audience, and as James Beard put it so well in his *Menus for Entertaining* in 1965, "there is no greater reward than pleasing your audience."

CHAPTER I

On-Your-Feet Entertaining— Stand and Nibble

✳ ✳ ✳

The Classic Cocktail Party

Wine Tasting

Open House

✳

WHO NEEDS AN EXCUSE? Let's throw a party! Let's get a group of people together, let's laugh, let's have some fun. Bringing a diverse group of people together can be one of the most satisfying forms of entertaining. Many people are intimidated by having a houseful of guests but it's easy and fun, and we've put together three ideas for you to make the party flow.

The most important element to entertaining a crowd is to be organized and to do all your food preparation in advance. With twelve to forty people all wanting a bit of your time and a chance to chat with you, you won't be able to handle lots of last-minute preparations. You need to be busy watching out for your guests' immediate needs–refilling their drinks and replenishing trays and platters of food. We have written all the menus to give you easy guidelines for do-ahead work.

We offer three menus for on-your-feet entertaining. The first is a Classic Cocktail Party or, perhaps we should say, a classy cocktail party. We give you marvelous drink recipes (including a classic martini) and then some delightful nibbles to keep your guests sane, sober, and well fed.

A Wine Tasting is a fun, relaxed, and casual way to bring a group of people together. We have planned the menu for twelve, but you can go for a larger group if your wine budget allows, or, better yet, ask each guest to bring a bottle. We recommend some specific wines in the introduction to the menu. The main goal of the menu is to offer some wine-friendly foods, some for whites, some for reds–delicious dips and spreads and a wonderful grilled lamb.

The third party style we offer is the Open House. Like the Wine Tasting, this event is more casual than a Classic Cocktail Party. The times for an open house are more open-ended, with people coming and going and mingling as their day and time allow. This menu can also be increased in number of servings if you want to invite the whole neighborhood, as well as your family. The foods are a fun mixture with a Middle Eastern accent and some incredible chocolate-dipped macaroons.

The one other element that makes a large party great is a great mix of people. Vary your invitation list. Invite some old friends you know well, and some new ones, or ones you've been wanting to know better. Mix the office crowd with the church crowd, or your neighbors with your college buddies. This is when the fun really starts.

If you follow our simple organizing plans for the next three menus and spice up your guest list, you can throw a party your friends will never forget, and you'll have a lot of fun doing it.

Classic Cocktail Party

SERVES 20 TO 25

❊ ❊ ❊

THE CLASSIC MARTINI

CHILLED GRAPEFRUIT VODKA
(not pictured)

FRESH FRUIT SPRITZER

ROSEMARY ROASTED PECANS

BLUE CHEESE SHORTBREADS
(not pictured)

WHITE BEAN DIP WITH GARLIC

CELERY WITH SPICY ASIAN
PEANUT BUTTER
(not pictured)

LOX ON RYE WITH
ONION-CAPER MAYONNAISE

❊

Suggested wine:
CHARDONNAY

Other beverages:
SPARKLING WATER

❋ *PLANNING AHEAD* ❋

- ◉ 2 to 3 weeks in advance, make and freeze pecans.

- ◉ 1 week in advance, make grapefruit vodka. Make and refrigerate onion-caper mayonnaise.

- ◉ 3 days in advance, make shortbreads.

- ◉ 1 day in advance, make and refrigerate bean dip. Strain grapefruit vodka back into vodka bottle, and store in freezer.

- ◉ The morning of the party, refresh pecans. Make spicy peanut butter, and cut celery. Set up bar.

- ◉ 2 to 3 hours in advance, prepare twists of lemon, put olives on toothpicks, and place in separate glasses on bar, ready for martinis. Squeeze or purée juice and cut garnishes for fruit spritzers; set on bar.

- ◉ 1 to 2 hours in advance, assemble and refrigerate lox appetizers. Stuff peanut butter into celery. Arrange and set out shortbreads and bean dip.

ARE YOU READY to invite twenty-five people to your home? The game plan is laid out, using a menu designed for you to enjoy your guests. There is no last-minute cooking or assembly. With some advanced planning, this party is guaranteed to go smoothly. Our menu, primarily vegetarian by design, combines international flavors and bold tastes. Cocktails, assertive in their own right, need to be accompanied by assertive foods. How can you miss with flavors like blue cheese, garlic, rosemary, ginger, lox, and onions? Your guests will notice and love the food!

Before the day of the party, think about where you want to set up the bar. Do you have a counter that will work, or a kitchen table that you can drape with an attractive cloth? Or is there another table that will allow guests to move about? You will also want to select platters and glassware. For this menu, it would be good to have two bowls for the pecans; two plates for the shortbreads; one bowl for the bean dip and one basket or large bowl for the bread, pita chips, and/or bagel chips; one or two platters for the stuffed celery; and two platters for the lox on rye. You don't need matching serving ware–here's a chance to be creative, and mix and match. You do need to have enough glassware. The last thing you want to do during your party is wash used glasses. If you do not own a plentiful supply of the kinds you need, borrow extras or consider renting. Not only is renting inexpensive but the returns only need to be rinsed, not cleaned. This is a huge timesaver for the host. Besides, if you inherited your great-aunt's crystal wineglasses, save them for a sit-down dinner where the chance of breakage is minimized.

To avoid last-minute errands, be sure to shop for groceries several days ahead of time. Think about buying flowers, plenty of cocktail napkins, and perhaps some decorative toothpicks for the martini olives. You'll want to serve wine as well, such as the Chardonnay suggested for this menu. Some folks steer clear of hard liquor, but do like a glass of wine. And for the non-drinkers, you'll have Fresh Fruit Spritzers or sparkling water. We typically figure on two or three drinks per person, but you may need to adjust this quantity, based on the crowd you invite.

If you make the recipes as designed, you'll have plenty of cocktail food for twenty to twenty-five guests. You can set out the serving dishes in various locations, or walk around with them–it's an easy way to greet and visit with guests.

Hey, remember to invite your guests!!! Are you sending invitations, or calling your friends? In either case we'd do it three weeks to one month ahead. Do ask for an RSVP; we prefer it to regrets only.

When the last guest has gone, pour yourself a drink, find a comfortable chair, put up your feet (for a bit!), and smile.

❋

The Classic Martini

SERVES I

FOR MARTINI AFICIONADOS, this is the all-time before-dinner cocktail. Ideally, it is served "straight up" in a stemmed martini glass. Alternatively, pour the unshaken liquor over ice cubes in an old-fashioned glass.

¼ cup dry gin
1 to 2 teaspoons dry vermouth
About 1 cup ice cubes or cracked (not crushed) ice
Twist of lemon peel or 1 or 2 pimiento-stuffed
   olives on a pick

Shake liquor with ice in a cocktail shaker or medium jar with lid for 10 to 15 seconds. Strain (pour through a small sieve if using jar as shaker) into martini glass. Garnish with the lemon peel or olives.

❋

Chilled Grapefruit Vodka

MAKES THIRTY 2-OUNCE SERVINGS

SERVE STRAIGHT from the freezer in small vodka glasses or pour over ice in old-fashioned glasses.

2 medium pink or white grapefruits (about
   1 pound each)
1 large bottle (1.75 liters) vodka

Using a citrus stripper or zester, or a vegetable peeler, remove zest (not white pith underneath) from grapefruits. In a 2-quart bottle or bowl, combine zest and vodka. Allow to stand, covered, for 4 to 7 days. Strain into vodka bottle. Store in freezer until serving.

❋

Fresh Fruit Spritzer

SERVES I

A COMBINATION of fresh fruit juice and a little sparkling water (seltzer) makes a very refreshing drink and allows a nonimbibing guest the opportunity to "work the crowd" with glass in hand, but without subverting his or her desire to avoid alcohol. Serve in a 12-ounce tumbler or highball glass.

Ice cubes or cracked ice
½ cup squeezed or puréed juice of fresh fruit,
   such as oranges, grapefruits, apples, various
   melons, strawberries, papayas, or mangos
½ cup sparkling water
Thin slices of same fruit, for garnish

Place ice in serving glass. Add juice and sparkling water and stir lightly to blend. Garnish with fruit slices.

Rosemary Roasted Pecans

SERVES 25

A BIG BOWL of roasted nuts is a favorite predinner nibble. It's also easy to prepare and serve. This version relies on aromatic rosemary, a touch of butter, and a spot of honey.

2 pounds whole pecans
½ stick (2 ounces) unsalted butter
¼ teaspoon cayenne pepper
1 tablespoon honey
½ cup chopped fresh rosemary
2 teaspoons salt

Preheat oven to 325°F. Divide pecans between 2 rimmed baking sheets. In a 1-quart saucepan over low heat, melt butter with cayenne pepper, honey, and rosemary. Allow rosemary to begin to sizzle in butter, then immediately pour butter over pecans, dividing it between the 2 pans. Sprinkle pecans with salt and toss with a spatula. Roast pecans until crisp and brown, about 25 minutes. Stir twice during baking. Let cool. To serve, divide among 2 bowls or place in 1 large (2-quart capacity) bowl.

Store pecans in tightly sealed freezer bags. In a very cold freezer (0°F) they will keep 3 to 4 months. If they have been frozen, it is nice to refresh them in a 300°F oven for 10 minutes before serving.

Blue Cheese Shortbreads

MAKES 9 TO 10 DOZEN SHORTBREADS

WE LOVE SHORTBREAD cookies and came up with the idea of substituting blue cheese for some of the butter in classic shortbread. The results are spectacular—the shortbreads are easy to make, store well, and taste great with our cocktails. We give directions using a food processor. An electric mixer or pastry blender will work just as well, but first use a knife to mince the parsley. A blender is not the right tool for this task.

2¼ cups all-purpose flour, plus more for dusting
6 sprigs fresh parsley, with about 2 inches of stems
2 sticks (8 ounces) unsalted butter, 30 minutes
    at room temperature, cut into small cubes
8 ounces blue cheese, crumbled (see Cook's Notes)
¾ cup (about 6 ounces) slivered, blanched
    almonds

In a food processor fitted with the metal blade, place flour and parsley. Process until parsley is well minced into flour. Remove lid, and distribute butter and cheese evenly over flour mixture. Use pulse button to mix just until a dough begins to form. It is better to gather dough into a mass with your hands than to run machine until a ball forms. Place dough on a large sheet of plastic wrap, flatten into a disk, and cover completely with plastic wrap. Refrigerate for 1 hour before rolling out.

Preheat oven to 350°F. Place dough in center of a lightly floured work surface and dust top of dough with flour. Lightly flour a rolling pin, and roll dough ¼ inch thick. Cut out shortbreads with a 1¼-inch-diameter cookie cutter (round, scalloped-edge round, star, or whatever shape you choose) and place ½ inch apart on ungreased baking sheets. Gather unused pieces of dough, dust with flour, reroll, and cut out until all dough is used. Lightly press a piece of almond onto top center of each cookie. Bake until lightly browned at edges, about 25 minutes. You'll need to bake the cookies in batches; refrigerate unbaked cookies until ready to bake. Cool on wire racks. Divide among 2 serving plates, or place on 1 large platter.

COOK'S NOTES

⤙ *There are many types of blue cheese—American blue, Danish blue, French Roquefort, Gorgonzola. All will work fine in this recipe. One of our favorites is Maytag blue cheese (yep, the same Maytag as the washing machines). Produced in Iowa, it has a wonderful flavor and texture. You can even mail-order it!*

⤙ *These shortbreads freeze well unbaked. Roll and cut out the cookies, layer between sheets of waxed paper, and freeze in a covered container. You can make them up to 1 month ahead. Bake from a frozen state, allowing for a slightly longer baking time. Alternatively, baked shortbreads will keep at room temperature for up to 3 days in a covered tin. Layer them between sheets of waxed paper or foil.*

※
White Bean Dip with Garlic
SERVES 25

HEY, GARLIC LOVERS, if you can fall out of bed, you can make this dip. It might take you 10 minutes. And can you believe it's good for you? A great amount of cocktail food is full of fat, but not this dip, so serve this happily to your guests.

- 2 cans (15 ounces each) small white beans (see Cook's Notes)
- 5 cloves garlic, peeled
- 2 tablespoons freshly squeezed lemon juice (about 1 lemon)
- 5 tablespoons extra-virgin olive oil
- ½ teaspoon salt
- Freshly ground black pepper, to taste
- 1 Roma tomato, seeded and diced, for garnish
- 2 large bags pita bread chips or 4 small bags bagel chips

Rinse beans under cold running water in a colander and allow to drain. Place garlic cloves in a food processor filled with the metal blade or in a blender and mince. Add beans and process to purée. Add lemon juice, olive oil, salt, and pepper, and purée until mixture forms a good consistency for dipping. Taste and add more oil, lemon juice, salt, or pepper as desired.

Place in a serving bowl, and garnish with diced tomato. Accompany with pita bread chips or bagel chips.

COOK'S NOTES
⤙ *For canned beans use small navy beans, cannellini beans, or small lima beans.*

Celery with Spicy Asian Peanut Butter

MAKES 80 TO 90 HORS D'OEUVRES

DO YOU REMEMBER when your mom fixed celery stuffed with cream cheese or peanut butter? For a great cocktail nibble, we took Skippy Super Chunk peanut butter and mixed it with ginger root, garlic, soy sauce, and sesame oil to create a fabulous Asian peanut butter to stuff into chunks of celery. Our guests made a joke about Skippy, and we said, "You bet!"

> 5 slices fresh ginger root (about the size of a quarter), peeled
> 2 scallions with green part, cut into ½-inch lengths
> 3 large cloves garlic, peeled
> 1 tablespoon granulated sugar
> 1 teaspoon red pepper flakes
> 2 cups super chunk peanut butter
> 4 tablespoons low-sodium soy sauce
> 2 tablespoons Asian sesame oil
> 1 large stalk celery (1½ to 2 pounds)

In a food processor fitted with the metal blade, place ginger, scallions, garlic, sugar, and red pepper flakes. Process until ingredients are finely minced. Add peanut butter, soy sauce, and sesame oil. Process until all ingredients are combined. Place in a small mixing bowl, cover, and set aside at room temperature (see Cook's Notes).

Prepare celery by trimming off tops, bottom core, and white portion of ribs. Use a vegetable peeler to remove strings from back of ribs. This isn't as necessary on the inner, more tender ribs, but makes for a nicer texture on the outer ribs (hey, we're picky!). Wash and dry celery. Cut ribs, straight across or on a slight angle (kind of an Asian look) into 1-inch-long chunks. Place in a plastic bag, seal, and refrigerate until ready to stuff.

Stuff celery 1 to 2 hours ahead of serving. Use a table knife to spread peanut butter into celery ribs. Smooth top or leave it more textured. If you feel like getting fancy, use a pastry bag and medium star tip to pipe peanut butter rosettes into each chunk of celery. Arrange stuffed celery on 1 or 2 platters, cover, and keep at room temperature until serving.

COOK'S NOTES

➤ *If you don't own a food processor, borrow one! No, this can also be done by hand or in a mixer, but first you'll need to mince the ginger, scallions, and garlic. For hand mixing, use a large bowl and a large, heavy spoon (and a strong arm!).*

➤ *Refrigerating the Asian peanut butter seems to diminish the bright ginger and chili flavors. We recommend making the peanut butter the day of the party. It's so quick to make that washing the food processor workbowl takes longer than combining the ingredients!*

Lox on Rye with
Onion-Caper Mayonnaise

MAKES 50 TO 60 HORS D'OEUVRES

LOX ARE THE DARLINGS of the salmon set. This delicately cured, tender fish is not inexpensive, but a little goes a long way. For this nibble, we place the slices on small rye squares, then gild the lily with a dollop of onion-caper mayonnaise.

1 cup mayonnaise
3 tablespoons capers, drained
⅓ cup finely diced sweet yellow onion
Freshly ground black pepper, to taste
Sliced rye bread (see Cook's Notes)
1 pound lox
4 sprigs fresh dill, for garnish (optional)

In a small bowl, mix mayonnaise, capers, onion, and pepper to taste. Refrigerate, covered, until ready to use.

Cut rye slices into 1½-inch squares. Cut lox slices the same size or a little smaller.

Place a lox slice on each rye slice and top with about ½ teaspoon onion-caper mayonnaise. Divide among 2 platters, garnish with dill sprigs (if using), and serve within an hour after assembling.

COOK'S NOTES

There are lots of possibilities for rye breads. Cocktail rye, a classic choice for this preparation, is often hard and dry. We suggest you find the best sliced rye and cut to the correct size.

Wine Tasting

SERVES 12

✳ ✳ ✳

MARINATED GOAT CHEESE
CURED OLIVES
Suggested wine: PINOT GRIGIO

✳

SMOKED SALMON PÂTÉ
(not pictured)
Suggested wine: PINOT GRIS OR
CHARDONNAY

✳

SAVORY WALNUT BISCOTTI
Suggested wine: PINOT NOIR

✳

CHARCOAL-GRILLED LAMB KEBOBS
CURED OLIVES
Suggested wine: ZINFANDEL OR
CABERNET SAUVIGNON

✳

ESPRESSO SHORTBREADS
Suggested beverage: COFFEE

✳

❋ PLANNING AHEAD ❋

- 2 to 3 weeks in advance, bake and freeze biscotti and shortbread.

- 1 to 2 weeks in advance, make and refrigerate goat cheese.

- 1 day in advance, prepare and refrigerate salmon pâté. Marinate lamb kebobs.

- The morning of the party, remove shortbread from freezer and thaw at room temperature.

- 3 to 4 hours before serving, remove goat cheese from refrigerator.

- 2 hours prior to grilling, remove lamb from refrigerator.

- Remove salmon pâté from refrigerator 1 hour before serving. Refresh biscotti in a preheated 300°F oven for 10 minutes.

- 40 minutes before grilling lamb, prepare fire.

BRINGING FRIENDS together for a wine tasting is a great way to learn about new wines and experience them with different foods. Our wine suggestions are just that. Your local wine merchant may recommend other wines to accompany the dishes on this menu. We have chosen foods that will compliment both white and red wines. If you prefer one or the other, change your menu accordingly. There are good possibilities from other menus in this book. White Bean Dip with Garlic (page 19) is terrific with crisp white wines, and Really Good Meatballs (page 36) are wonderful with a full-bodied red.

Guests may bring a wine, but it is wise to give them a couple of suggestions that work with the menu.

Plan to set the various foods and wines at different "stations" so people can linger for a time with each specific food and wine. You might start the Marinated Goat Cheese with its accompanying wine in the kitchen. (Everyone always congregates in the kitchen anyway.) Then you can move guests to the living room or dining room for the next courses and wines, and then to an area where they can relax with coffee and Espresso Shortbread.

It is not essential, but if you have enough glasses, it is nice to change glasses between the white and red wines. Otherwise, you might want to rinse them out. Don't be offended if some guests don't finish all their wine from a specific course. Four different wines are a lot for some to handle. Have water available if guests need a break between tastings. As an elegant touch, prepare a simple menu card that guests can read when they first arrive so they know the order of the evening.

Stack plenty of cocktail napkins at each station and small plates by the kebobs. The cured olives we recommend with the goat cheese and kebobs can be bought at a specialty-food store or deli. Many large supermarkets offer some good olives as well.

Enjoy your evening. Raise a glass to toast fine wines, good food, and good friends. *Salud!*

Marinated Goat Cheese

SERVES 15 TO 20

YOU'VE SEEN THIS already prepared in gourmet shops and fancy delis, but you can make it yourself. You won't believe how easy it is. You just need to plan ahead a bit, so you can give it 1 to 2 weeks marinating time. There are many different goat cheeses on the market. Buy one that is plain, without added flavorings, and firmer as opposed to softer. The marinated cheese is wonderful to have on hand when unexpected guests drop by.

1 pound goat cheese

3 bay leaves

1 teaspoon crushed red pepper

20 whole black peppercorns, slightly crushed

1 teaspoon dried rosemary

1 teaspoon dried thyme

2 cups extra-virgin olive oil, or as needed to
    cover cheese (see Cook's Notes)

2 loaves French bread, sliced

Choose a clean 1-quart jar or container in which you can layer cheese and cover it with oil.

Cut cheese into disks about ½ inch thick. You may have to cut disks in half if cheese comes as a wide log. Rinse your knife in hot water once or twice to help make clean slices and prevent crumbling.

Layer cheese slices in container and add bay leaves, red pepper, peppercorns, rosemary, and thyme. Cover cheese completely with olive oil. Cover jar tightly and place in refrigerator until ready to serve.

Remove cheese from refrigerator 3 to 4 hours before serving so it comes to room temperature. Remove pieces from oil and place on a serving dish with an edge. Some olive oil will pool in bottom of dish. Accompany with slices of French bread arranged on a plate or in a basket.

COOK'S NOTES

You can use some very expensive olive oils to marinate the cheese, but we have found that Bertolli's extra-virgin is just fine. When the cheese is gone, don't throw away the olive oil. It makes wonderful salad dressings. You can strain it if you wish, but the bits of cheese and herbs are delicious.

Smoked Salmon Pâté

SERVES 12 TO 20

MOST SUPERMARKETS carry "cured" smoked salmon, which is usually a fairly dark color and firm texture compared with lox. Combining a little smoked salmon with cooked fresh salmon makes for an interesting taste treat.

12 ounces fresh salmon fillet or steaks
  (see Cook's Notes)
4 ounces firm smoked salmon
1 tablespoon vegetable oil
1 large yellow onion (about 8 ounces), peeled
  and coarsely chopped
8 ounces cream cheese
½ teaspoon salt
Freshly ground black pepper, to taste
½ teaspoon hot-pepper sauce
½ cup minced fresh parsley
2 tablespoons capers, drained
1 long, thin loaf crusty bread (baguette) or
  1 box crackers of your choice

Fill a 3-quart sauté pan or a 10-inch frying pan with enough water to cover piece(s) of fresh salmon. Bring water to a boil, slide in the fresh salmon skin side up (if fillet), and simmer, uncovered, for about 10 minutes for each inch of thickness. For example, if fish is 1 inch thick, simmer for about 10 minutes. An instant-read thermometer inserted in center of fish should register 140°F or more. With a slotted spatula, remove fish from water and slide onto a paper towel–covered plate. Cool for 5 minutes, then peel off skin and discard.

Refrigerate salmon for 2 hours or more.

When ready to make pâté, remove any skin and obvious bones from smoked salmon. Cut into thumbnail-size pieces and set aside. Heat oil in a 3-quart saucepan or a 10-inch frying pan over medium-low heat. Add onion and cook until soft but not browned, about 5 minutes. Remove onion to a plate and spread out to cool for 5 minutes.

Remove any obvious bones from cooled poached salmon, break into several pieces, and place in a food processor fitted with the metal blade. Add cooked onion, cream cheese, salt, a few grinds of black pepper, and hot-pepper sauce. Process until ingredients are well blended, scraping down workbowl once or twice. Add smoked salmon, parsley, and capers. Pulse a few times to break smoked salmon into small bits and blend ingredients (do not run machine constantly to avoid puréeing smoked salmon and capers). Scrape pâté into a medium mixing bowl, give it a few turns with a rubber spatula to blend ingredients, taste for seasoning, and adjust if desired. Place in a serving bowl, cover, and refrigerate. Remove from refrigerator about 1 hour before serving.

If using bread, slice very thinly. Arrange bread slices or crackers on a plate or in a small basket and place next to pâté on serving table.

COOK'S NOTES

Salmon fillets from the tail are thinner and cook more quickly than center-cut fillets and have no bones, making them a good choice for this pâté.

Savory Walnut Biscotti

MAKES 30 TO 34 BISCOTTI

BISCOTTI HAVE hit the top of the charts on America's food popularity list. While putting together this wine-tasting menu, we thought, why not a savory version? We removed all but a bit of sugar, then added cayenne, fresh rosemary, Parmesan cheese, and crispy walnuts. Your greatest challenge will be keeping the kitchen nibblers away from these long enough to get them to the table.

Butter or nonstick cooking spray, for coating
   baking sheet
1 stick (4 ounces) unsalted butter
2 tablespoons chopped fresh rosemary
1/4 teaspoon cayenne pepper
3 large eggs
1 tablespoon granulated sugar
2 1/2 cups all-purpose flour
1/2 cup cornmeal
1 1/2 teaspoons baking powder
1/2 teaspoon salt
1/3 cup grated Parmesan cheese
   (see Cook's Notes)
1 cup finely chopped walnuts

Preheat oven to 350°F. Butter a baking sheet or spray with nonstick cooking spray. In a 1-quart saucepan over low heat, melt butter with rosemary and cayenne. Let cool slightly.

In a large mixing bowl, beat eggs and sugar until well blended, using a heavy-duty stand mixer or a handheld electric mixer. Add melted butter and blend. Add dry ingredients, then cheese and walnuts. If using a stand mixer, knead dough until well blended. Or, use your hands to knead dough on a lightly floured work surface until well blended. (Mixture has a tendency to be crumbly; complete kneading helps dough stay together.)

Form dough into 2 logs, each about 10 inches long. Place logs on a prepared baking sheet 3 inches apart and bake until light, sandy brown, about 30 minutes. Cool for 5 minutes. Carefully remove 1 log to a cutting board, and slice about 1/2 inch thick with a serrated knife. Return slices to baking sheet. Repeat with other log. Biscotti will crumble slightly at this point, but if you work slowly and carefully, you will minimize it.

Bake biscotti until a light, sandy color shows on sides, about 20 minutes. Remove from oven and cool completely. Arrange on a platter to serve.

COOK'S NOTES

We prefer good imported Parmigiano-Reggiano. If it's not available, buy the best dry-grating cheese you can find and grate it yourself. Dry Sonoma Jack is an excellent choice.

To store the biscotti, tightly seal in lock-top plastic bags. They will keep at room temperature for 3 to 4 days. They can be frozen for 1 month. Refresh in a preheated 300°F oven for 10 minutes.

Charcoal-Grilled Lamb Kebobs

SERVES 12 TO 16

TOO MANY SPREADS and dips leave some people craving something more substantial during stand-up events. These grilled kebobs will satisfy the most confirmed meat lovers in the crowd. You can bone and trim the lamb yourself or ask a butcher to do the job for you.

> 1 boneless leg of lamb, trimmed of skin,
>   gristle, and fat, cut into 1-inch pieces
>   (about 3 pounds prepared)
> ½ cup plus 2 tablespoons olive oil
> ¼ cup plus 2 tablespoons red wine vinegar
> Freshly ground black pepper, to taste
> ¼ teaspoon ground cinnamon
> ½ teaspoon ground cumin
> ¼ cup chopped fresh basil or 1 tablespoon
>   dried basil
> About 18 bamboo skewers, 6 inches or longer,
>   soaked in water 1 hour, or about 18 metal
>   skewers of similar length
> Salt, to taste
> 4 sprigs fresh basil or parsley, for garnish

Place lamb pieces in a 1-gallon lock-top plastic bag. In a small mixing bowl combine olive oil, vinegar, black pepper, cinnamon, cumin, and basil and pour into bag. Squeeze air out of bag, seal, and place in a 9-by-13-inch or similar baking dish to catch juices if bag leaks. Refrigerate 24 hours, turning bag over several times.

Remove bag from refrigerator 2 hours before grilling time. Drain marinade from lamb and thread pieces onto presoaked bamboo skewers or metal skewers. Salt lightly. Grill over a hot charcoal fire or gas grill (page 108) about 5 minutes, turning once, until meat is medium-rare or as you prefer it. Slide lamb off skewers onto a platter garnished with basil or parsley sprigs. Have a small container of wooden toothpicks in the center of the platter for guests to serve themselves, and a small bowl for used picks close by.

COOK'S NOTES

Use a preheated broiler to cook the skewered lamb if outdoor grilling is impractical. Pour cold water to a depth of ½ inch in bottom of broiler pan to prevent excess smoking.

Espresso Shortbreads

MAKES ABOUT 40 SHORTBREADS

THESE SHORTBREADS have the intense flavor and aroma of really good espresso. Make them with good-quality ground espresso that you have ground yourself or ask a local coffee store to grind the beans for you. Use your favorite cookie cutters to cut out shapes—we cut our shortbreads in the shape of dog bones once. A playful shape perks up the conversation when dessert comes along.

  2 sticks (8 ounces) unsalted butter, 30 minutes
      at room temperature, cut into small cubes
  ⅔ cup powdered sugar
  ¼ teaspoon salt
  1¾ cups all-purpose flour, plus more
      for dusting
  ¼ cup fresh (unbrewed) extrafine ground espresso
      roast coffee

In a large mixing bowl, beat butter with powdered sugar on low speed of an electric mixer for 30 seconds. Add salt, flour, and ground espresso. Continue mixing on low speed, occasionally scraping down sides of bowl with a rubber spatula, until dough just comes together. It should look dry.

Turn dough onto a lightly floured work surface, and dust top of dough with flour. Roll out ¼ inch thick. Cut shortbreads with a cookie cutter of your choice. Place 1 inch apart on ungreased baking sheets. Gather unused pieces, lightly dust with flour only if needed, then reroll dough and cut out cookies until all dough is used.

Refrigerate for 1 hour.

Preheat oven to 300°F. Bake shortbreads until firm, 25 to 30 minutes. Because the dough is dark, it is hard to tell when the cookies are done. Feel them for firmness, and pay attention to the aroma. At about 25 minutes, the smell of coffee should be noticeable—and delightful. Remove from sheets to wire racks to cool.

COOK'S NOTES

➤ *These shortbreads can be made up to 3 months ahead and frozen. Pack between sheets of waxed paper and freeze in a plastic freezer container. Thaw at room temperature. You can also make them up to 1 week ahead and store in a tightly covered tin at room temperature.*

➤ *If you want to make plain shortbread, use 2 cups all-purpose flour and eliminate espresso grounds.*

Open House

SERVES 20 TO 25

* * *

MEDITERRANEAN TOMATO TARTS

CUCUMBER YOGURT DIP WITH
PITA TOASTS AND FRESH VEGETABLES

MINIATURE CORN MUFFINS WITH
BLACK FOREST HAM

ROASTED NEW POTATOES TOSSED
WITH OLIVE OIL AND FRESH HERBS

REALLY GOOD MEATBALLS
(not pictured)

COCONUT MACAROONS DIPPED
IN CHOCOLATE

*

Suggested wines:
PINOT GRIGIO (WHITE),
PINOT NOIR OR
VALPOLICELLA (RED)

Other beverages:
SPARKLING WATER, COFFEE, TEA

✳ *PLANNING AHEAD* ✳

- ◎ 2 to 3 weeks in advance, make and freeze corn muffins. Make shells for tomato tarts and freeze unbaked.

- ◎ 2 days in advance, make and refrigerate yogurt dip. Make pita toasts. Make meatballs and refrigerate. Make and refrigerate sauce for meatballs. Make and refrigerate flavored mayonnaise for muffins.

- ◎ 1 day in advance, make macaroons.

- ◎ The morning of the party, cut and refrigerate vegetables for yogurt dip. Bake shells for tomato tarts and assemble ingredients for tart filling. Make potatoes.

- ◎ 2 hours in advance, assemble corn muffins with ham and mayonnaise.

- ◎ 1 hour in advance, fill tomato tarts and bake.

- ◎ 20 minutes in advance, warm meatballs and potatoes. Set out sauce.

WHOA, NELLIE . . . there are a lot of people coming. Well, yeah, but here are the plans, laid out ready for you to tackle. Just follow along. Open houses typically involve entertaining a number of people, so to pull this off, you have to be organized. The great part about giving a party this way is that all your hosting obligations can be taken care of at once. Most open houses occur at Christmastime, or for a graduation, or for showing off a new home. Written invitations sold at stationery stores are recommended. You can find fill-in-the-blank versions in which you can write date, time, place, and other details. An RSVP is optional. If it's important to know how many guests are coming, then ask for a reply. People like to know what they might expect, so state on the invitation whether the event is a light buffet, or cocktails and hors d'oeuvres, or even a dessert buffet if that is your menu. We would call this menu a light buffet.

Our menu was created to offer substantial nibbles with great tastes. Your vegetarian guests will be delighted to try the tomato tart, munch on pita toasts and vegetables served with a tangy yogurt dip, and savor the herbed roasted potatoes. And for guests who graze on anything, the corn muffins with ham and the meatballs will surely be a hit. We doubt you'll have any macaroons left over. Just wait until you taste them!

Here's what you will need for serving pieces: one or two 12-inch-diameter platters for the tomato tarts; a decorative bowl for the dip, a basket or bowl for the pita toasts, and a platter for the vegetables; a large platter or tray for the miniature muffins; a platter or a shallow, wide bowl for the potatoes. If you have a chafing dish or can borrow one, this is ideal for the potatoes and meatballs, to keep them warm. A small bowl or sauceboat and little ladle can be used for the accompanying sauce. The macaroons will look great on a decorative serving plate.

You'll also need little plates, small forks, and plenty of cocktail napkins and glasses. Have some coffee cups and saucers on hand for those wanting coffee or tea. If you have enough small plates to mix and match, then use your own; otherwise borrow from family and friends. Sturdy paper plates are certainly an option.

An open house is a great occasion to decorate with flowers—on tables where you are serving food and wine, in the kitchen, and in the bathroom. The decor can fit the occasion. At Christmastime your decorated tree, the glow of candles, and a crackling fire in the fireplace will certainly set a festive mood.

Mediterranean Tomato Tarts

MAKES TWO 11-INCH TARTS
OR 40 SMALL WEDGES

WE'VE TAKEN THE FLAVORS of the Mediterranean—olives, tomatoes, and basil—and packaged them in a biscuit crust. This tart relies on a few, simple ingredients, so they must be good. Find the best tomatoes the market has to offer, and look for a good goat cheese, either French or American.

4 cups all-purpose flour, plus more for dusting

4 teaspoons baking powder

½ teaspoon baking soda

½ teaspoon salt

1 stick (4 ounces) unsalted butter, very cold,
    plus more for coating pan

1⅓ cups buttermilk

1 pound Kalamata olives, pitted
    (see Cook's Notes)

1 pound fresh tomatoes (about 2 medium),
    thinly sliced

½ pound red onion (about 1 medium),
    peeled and thinly sliced

10 ounces soft goat cheese, crumbled

¼ cup extra-virgin olive oil

⅔ cups chopped fresh basil, plus 1 sprig
    for garnish

Preheat oven to 450°F. Lightly butter two 11-inch tart pans with removable bottoms. In a large mixing bowl, combine dry ingredients. Cut butter into small pieces and add to flour. Using your fingertips, rub butter into dry ingredients until mixture resembles texture of oatmeal. Slowly add buttermilk, stirring briskly with a fork. Mix just until buttermilk is incorporated.

Turn mixture onto a floured work surface. Divide into 2 equal pieces. Press each piece into a prepared pan, using your knuckles to press dough to outer edges. If dough offers too much resistance, let it rest for a few minutes and proceed after it has relaxed. Bake tart shells until crisp and brown, about 20 minutes. Set aside until using.

Lower oven temperature to 375°F. Chop pitted olives and sprinkle evenly over tart shells. Top with sliced tomatoes, sliced onion, and crumbled goat cheese. Drizzle tarts evenly with olive oil. Bake until tomatoes have softened and cheese is just beginning to brown, about 20 minutes. Remove from oven and sprinkle tarts with chopped basil. Let sit 15 minutes.

Remove sides of tart pans and gently slide tarts onto a cutting board. Cut in small wedges with a sharp chef's knife. Serve from cutting board or transfer to 1 or 2 platters. Garnish with whole basil sprigs.

COOK'S NOTES

Most Mediterranean-style olives are not available pitted. To pit, place several at a time on a cutting board and hit with the blunt side of a chef's knife or a cleaver. The pits will easily come free.

The crusts can be frozen, unbaked, for 2 to 3 weeks. Wrap tightly in a couple layers of plastic wrap. Bake from a frozen state.

Cucumber Yogurt Dip with Pita Toasts and Fresh Vegetables

SERVES 20 TO 25

THIS RECIPE is a variation on what you might know as *tzatziki,* a traditional Greek appetizer. It's a simple recipe to make ahead and serve with pita toasts and fresh vegetables. The dip is best made up to two days ahead to allow the flavors to meld. Choose your favorite vegetables as an accompaniment.

Dip
1 cup plain low-fat yogurt
1 cup sour cream
4 cloves garlic, peeled and minced
¼ cup minced fresh mint (see Cook's Notes)
3 tablespoons extra-virgin olive oil
¼ teaspoon salt
Freshly ground black pepper, to taste
1 large cucumber (14 to 16 ounces), peeled,
    cut in half lengthwise, and seeds removed

Pita Toasts
12 pita breads, white or whole wheat, or
    a combination

Vegetables
3 large red, yellow, or orange bell peppers,
    seeded, deveined, and cut into long, thin strips
1 pound baby carrots
8 ribs celery
1 teaspoon salt
1 to 1½ pounds broccoli or 1 head cauliflower,
    cut into florets (see Cook's Notes)

To make dip, in a medium mixing bowl, combine yogurt, sour cream, garlic, mint, olive oil, salt, and a few grinds of pepper. Set aside. Coarsely grate cucumber and place in a strainer. Use your hands or the back of a spoon to squeeze as much liquid as possible from cucumber, discarding liquid. Add cucumber to yogurt mixture, and stir to combine. Place dip in a serving bowl, cover, and refrigerate until serving time.

To prepare pita toasts, preheat oven to 350°F. Cut each pita bread into eighths, then split apart pocket of each wedge. Place wedges in a single layer on 2 rimmed baking sheets. Don't crowd pita wedges; it's better to bake them in 2 batches. Bake until lightly browned and crisp, 10 to 15 minutes. Let cool. Store, covered, at room temperature for up to 5 days. Serve in a bowl or basket.

To prepare vegetables, arrange peppers and baby carrots on a serving platter large enough to hold all the vegetables. Set aside. Prepare celery by trimming off tops and white portion of ribs. Use a vegetable peeler to remove strings from back of ribs. Wash and dry celery. Cut celery into half lengthwise, then cut into 3-inch-long sticks. Arrange on serving platter and set aside. Bring a large pot of water to a boil, and add 1 teaspoon salt. Add broccoli or cauliflower florets and cook 3 minutes. Drain, then immediately place vegetables in a large bowl of ice water to stop cooking process. Remove as soon as vegetables are cold, about 1 minute. Lay on paper towels to drain. Arrange on platter, cover with plastic wrap, and refrigerate until ready to serve.

COOK'S NOTES
➤ *Fresh mint can be found in most supermarkets year-round. If it is unavailable, substitute fresh dill or cilantro.*

~ We prefer to blanch broccoli and cauliflower rather than serve it raw. If you like broccoli and cauliflower raw, then skip the cooking directions. Just rinse the vegetables and arrange on a serving platter.

✳

Miniature Corn Muffins with Black Forest Ham

MAKES 50 TO 55 MUFFINS

HAM AND CORN BREAD, a classic combination, come together in miniature form. These bright yellow morsels look pretty on any hors d'oeuvre table.

Muffins

Butter or nonstick cooking spray, for coating pan
3 cups cornmeal (medium to fine grind)
1 cup all-purpose flour
2 teaspoons baking powder
1 teaspoon baking soda
1 tablespoon salt
½ teaspoon freshly ground black pepper
3 eggs, lightly beaten
½ stick (2 ounces) unsalted butter, melted and
    cooled slightly
2 cups plus 1 tablespoon sour cream
1 cup frozen corn kernels, defrosted

Sauce

4 ounces dried figs
¼ cup Dijon-style mustard
¼ cup mayonnaise
1 tablespoon sour cream

1 pound Black Forest or other good-quality ham,
    thinly sliced
½ small yellow onion (about 2 ounces), peeled
    and thinly sliced

Preheat oven to 400°F. Butter mini-muffin cups or coat with nonstick cooking spray.

In a large mixing bowl, combine dry ingredients. Add eggs, butter, 2 cups sour cream, and corn kernels, and stir until just combined. Spoon batter into mini-muffin cups, filling each to the top. Muffins will dome nicely as they bake. Bake until just beginning to brown, 12 to 13 minutes. Cool for 3 to 4 minutes. Remove from pan and cool completely on wire racks. Bake remaining muffins.

To make sauce, place figs in a small mixing bowl, add boiling water to cover, and let stand for 30 minutes. Drain in a colander and pat dry with paper towels. Mince figs and combine in a medium mixing bowl with mustard, mayonnaise, and 1 tablespoon of sour cream. Set aside.

To assemble muffins, cut ham slices in half. Slice each muffin in half horizontally so there is a top and a bottom. Place about ½ teaspoon sauce on both top and bottom. Fold ham slice once or twice so it fits on the muffin bottom; ham will hang slightly over edges of muffin. Place 2 or 3 onion slices on ham. If onion slices are too large, cut in halves or thirds. Top with muffin top, pressing down slightly. Arrange on a serving platter or tray.

COOK'S NOTES

~ *The muffins can be made ahead and stored in lock-top plastic bags for 3 days. They can also be frozen for 1 month. Thaw before using, and refresh, if possible, in a preheated 300°F oven.*

Roasted New Potatoes Tossed with Olive Oil and Fresh Herbs

SERVES 20 TO 25

UNUSUAL ON A BUFFET for an open house? We don't think so. It is fun to see homey, comfort foods mixed with fussier finger foods. Besides, for the cook's sake, balancing easy, do-ahead foods with some last-minute preparation is the only sane way to manage this type of entertaining.

4 pounds baby new potatoes
¾ cup extra-virgin olive oil (see Cook's Notes)
5 cloves garlic, peeled and minced
2 teaspoons salt
Freshly ground black pepper, to taste
2 tablespoons minced fresh rosemary
2 tablespoons minced fresh thyme

Preheat oven to 350°F. Wash potatoes, then prick with a fork in several places. Place potatoes in a single layer on 1 or 2 rimmed baking sheets. Roast until potatoes are crisp on the outside and tender when pierced with a fork, 1 to 1½ hours.

In a 2-quart saucepan, heat olive oil, garlic, salt, pepper, and fresh herbs until hot. Stir to dissolve salt, then remove from heat and set aside.

Cut potatoes in half and place in a large mixing bowl. Pour olive oil mixture over potatoes and toss gently to coat potatoes. Let sit at room temperature until ready to serve, up to 6 hours ahead. Place potatoes on an ovenproof serving platter or bowl, then warm, uncovered, in a preheated 300°F oven for 20 minutes.

COOK'S NOTES

🐟 *Here is an instance where a good-quality extra virgin olive oil makes sense. You can really taste the flavor. If a local specialty market stocks olive oil from Tuscany, try it. Some Tuscan olive oils have a peppery finish that would be great with the potatoes.*

🐟 *If, after tossing the potatoes with the oil mixture some is left at the bottom of the bowl, then save it. We keep the leftover oil refrigerated, then coat a chicken with it for roasting.*

🐟 *Keep two things in mind for serving and presentation. If possible, serve the potatoes warm, not hot, by using a chafing dish or a warming tray. Instead of heaping the potatoes in a bowl, think of serving them on a low, round platter arranged attractively in a spiral in a single layer.*

Really Good Meatballs

MAKES ABOUT 45 MEATBALLS

GUARANTEED TO BE one of the most popular items on your open house menu, these meatballs are equally tasty served warm or at room temperature. You may bake (and freeze) them weeks in advance or prepare them up to two days before your party and rewarm briefly. In either case, they will deliver a lot of enjoyment for very little last-minute attention from the cook.

Meatballs
½ cup uncooked white rice (not the "converted" type)
1½ pounds ground beef (see Cook's Notes)

8 ounces ground pork

1 small yellow onion (3 ounces), peeled and finely chopped

½ cup finely chopped parsley

2 tablespoons finely chopped fresh dill or 2 teaspoons dried dill

1 teaspoon salt

8 to 10 grinds black pepper

2 large eggs

1 tablespoon Dijon-style mustard

1 teaspoon anchovy paste

4 sprigs fresh dill or parsley, for garnish

Sauce

2 cups sour cream

½ cup buttermilk, or as needed

1 tablespoon Dijon-style mustard

½ cup chopped fresh dill or 2 tablespoons dried dill

1 teaspoon salt, or to taste

To make meatballs, bring 2 quarts water to a boil in a 3-quart saucepan. Add rice and boil for 10 minutes. Drain in a wire sieve and rinse with cold water to stop cooking. Shake as much water from rice as possible and set sieve over a bowl to drain for 5 minutes.

Place beef and pork in a 4-quart or larger mixing bowl. With a fork or chopstick, loosen and toss meats. Add cooked rice, onion, parsley, dill, salt, and pepper. In a small mixing bowl, beat together eggs, mustard, and anchovy paste. Pour egg mixture over meat and use a fork or chopstick to toss and mix until meat mixture seems uniform but not compacted.

Preheat oven to 425°F. Select two 9-by-13-inch or larger nonstick baking pans or line regular baking pans with aluminum foil to make cleanup easier. Using a spoon or small quick-release ice cream scoop, dip out mounds of meat mixture into your wet hands, 1 at a time. Roll into a round shape no larger than a golf ball and no smaller than a large grape. Arrange 1 inch apart on prepared pans. Bake in middle level of oven until lightly browned and an instant-read thermometer inserted in center of a meatball registers 160°F, 20 to 25 minutes.

To make sauce, in a medium bowl, mix sour cream with enough buttermilk to thin sour cream to the consistency of gravy. Add mustard, dill, and salt. Taste and adjust seasonings if desired.

Arrange meatballs on a platter and garnish with dill or parsley sprigs. Place sauce in a small bowl or sauceboat and serve alongside.

Cook's Notes

✒ *Use 2 pounds ground beef if not using the pork, or substitute ground veal for the pork.*

✒ *Cooked meatballs may be refrigerated, covered, for 3 days or frozen for 3 months. Thaw frozen meatballs 24 hours in the refrigerator. Warm in a preheated 300°F oven before serving.*

✳

Coconut Macaroons Dipped in Chocolate

MAKES 3 DOZEN MACAROONS

ANYONE WHO LOVES coconut and chocolate will adore these macaroons. They are surprisingly easy to prepare. Forget the electric mixer or food processor. These cookies are made in a saucepan using only a wooden spoon to stir the thick batter. You will need non-stick baking sheets. Once you have used nonstick baking sheets for cookies, you'll wonder why you used anything else. Macaroons don't freeze well, but they will keep in a covered container for 3 to 4 days. However, they are too good to be resisted. You'd better hide them until serving time!

½ cup light corn syrup
⅔ cup granulated sugar
2 teaspoons pure vanilla extract
¾ cup egg whites (about 5 large eggs), at room
    temperature
5 ⅓ cups (about 1 pound) firmly packed,
    shredded sweetened coconut (see Cook's Notes)
⅓ cup cake flour, sifted
8 ounces bittersweet or semisweet chocolate
1 teaspoon vegetable oil

Preheat oven to 350°F. Have ready 2 nonstick baking sheets.

In a heavy 4-quart saucepan, bring corn syrup to a boil. Swirl pan just above burner until you see uniform little bubbles. Remove from heat and add sugar, stirring with a wooden spoon. Return to heat and stir continu-ously to dissolve sugar; mixture will look grainy and white. Remove from heat and let sugar syrup cool for 4 minutes. Stir in vanilla, then briskly stir in egg whites until well mixed. Add coconut and cake flour, and mix just until flour is incorporated. Drop generous table-spoonfuls of batter, placed several inches apart, onto baking sheets.

Bake until toasty brown, 15 to 20 minutes. Remove immediately to wire racks, and cool completely. Bake additional batches until batter is used.

Break or cut chocolate into small chunks. Melt chocolate with vegetable oil in a double boiler over medium heat (see Cook's Notes). When most, but not all, of chocolate is melted, remove from heat and stir until smooth. Alternatively, chocolate can be melted in a microwave: Place chocolate and oil in a small glass bowl and cook, uncovered, on high power for 2 minutes. Remove, stir well, cook an additional 30 seconds, then stir again. Continue stirring to melt chocolate without additional cooking. Let cool about 5 minutes, stir again, then you are ready to dip cookies.

To dip macaroons, set 2 long sheets of waxed or parchment paper on a work surface. Dip about one-third of each macaroon into chocolate, so that chocolate coats both top and bottom. Place on waxed paper until choco-late hardens. Try to keep your fingers out of the choco-late. It makes dipping less messy; save finger licking for the end! Arrange on serving plate.

COOK'S NOTES
➤ In a well-stocked supermarket, you will probably find sweetened shredded coconut and angel flake coconut. For this recipe, you want to use shredded coconut. It keeps well, tightly sealed.

If you don't own a double boiler, you can use a heat-proof bowl placed over a medium saucepan. Bring 2 to 3 inches of water to a simmer in saucepan; set heatproof bowl on top, making sure water doesn't touch bottom of bowl; then proceed to melt chocolate.

Pour leftover melted chocolate onto waxed paper, allow to harden and save for future use.

CHAPTER 2

Buffets

✳ ✳ ✳

Soup and Bread Supper

Sports Buffet

✳

LINE UP! LET'S EAT! We love to eat buffet style. Our independent-minded natures welcome the chance to pick and choose from the variety offered, taking as much as we want of what we want. Buffets are great for the host as well. Without question, this is an easier form of entertaining than the sit-down dinner, and thus is suited for larger crowds. In its style, the buffet comes between the stand-up party and the sit-down dinner. Guests are standing to receive their food, but then sitting to eat, at tables, at the kitchen counter, on the living-room sofa, or in the family room. You can set tables if you have enough space or let people land where they may.

Buffets offer natural advantages for the host. Everything is served at once so no one is required to be a waitperson. There can be great flexibility with food. The only restriction in planning a buffet menu is to work with foods that can withstand being set out for the half hour to hour it will take everyone to get through the line, or to find a adequate heat source (hot plate or warming tray) to keep sensitive items warm.

Buffets can be casual or dressy in style. The two we offer in this chapter are definitely easy and relaxed. We envision serving the soups for the Soup and Bread Supper directly from the range. The remainder of the buffet can be set on the kitchen counter. It is a warm and cozy menu and just great for entertaining a few close friends.

A big television sports event is a natural for putting together a fun buffet. We offer some spice in a slightly Southwest-style menu that begins with a good salsa and dip and plenty of chips to get everybody through the game opener. The main part of the menu could be served at halftime (if there is one) or at the game's conclusion when armchair bets are being collected.

Many other menus in this book can easily become buffets–the Jewish-Style Brunch, the Easter Brunch, both outdoor entertaining menus, Thanksgiving, and Christmas. Don't hesitate to have your friends and family over if you don't think you have the space or energy to serve them all. Let them line up and let them eat!

Soup and Bread Supper

SERVES 8 TO 10

✳ ✳ ✳

CHICKEN AND CORN CHOWDER
(not pictured)

WINTER SQUASH SOUP

IRISH SODA BREAD

FRESH FRUIT AND CHEESE PLATTER

✳

Suggested wines:
LIGHT CHIANTI OR BEER

Other beverages:
COFFEE, TEA

✳

◉ 2 to 3 days in advance, make and refrigerate squash soup.

◉ 1 to 2 days in advance, make and refrigerate chowder.

◉ The day of the party, make bread.

◉ 1 hour before serving, arrange cheese and fruit (leave pears and apples whole) on a serving platter. Heat soup and chowder; warm soup bowls or mugs.

◉ 20 minutes before serving, warm bread and slice.

THIS IS A PERFECT menu for a relaxed fall or winter evening. The possibilities are broad: dinner in a mountain cabin after a day of skiing, friends joining you for an early Sunday dinner after a sports event, or Saturday evening before a play or movie. Our menu is hearty and homespun. The squash soup has a smoky-sweet quality, while the chowder is chunky with chicken and corn. Savory bread with currants and a hint of caraway is a perfect match for these soups. We love to finish a meal with seasonal fruit and a bite of cheese. Relaxed, casual entertaining is so much fun. It's too easy to forget that parties don't need to be productions. We think it's wonderful to serve this menu right from the kitchen–our guests usually end up there anyway!

　　Keep the soups right on the stove, set a basket of bread on the counter, place the fruit and cheese platter nearby, and you're set. Your friends can enjoy one bowl of soup, then come back to try the other. Have a plate and bowl ready for each person. Mugs are great because they sit on the plate without taking up a lot of room. Roll a soup spoon in a big napkin. Then your guests can settle anywhere. Gather around a fireplace, set floor cushions around a coffee table, or sit at the dining room table. This is entertaining at its best.

✳

Chicken and Corn Chowder

SERVES 10 TO 12

WE'LL STAND on our soapbox here and urge you to make this soup when fresh corn is available. It's terrific with the taste and texture of fresh corn. Frozen corn is an acceptable substitute in the late fall and winter when a hearty bowl of chowder tastes great. Making homemade chicken stock is easier than you think and the taste is incomparably better than anything you can buy canned. We give you a recipe here for making your own.

4 ears fresh corn or 3 cups frozen corn kernels
1 to 1¼ pounds boneless, skinless chicken breasts
1 rib celery with tops, cut into 2-inch lengths
3 tablespoons vegetable oil
1 large yellow onion (about 12 ounces), peeled and diced
1½ tablespoons curry powder
2 cups Chicken Stock (recipe follows) or 1 can (16 ounces) low-sodium chicken broth
4 medium red potatoes (about 2 pounds), peeled and cut into ½-inch dice
5 sprigs fresh thyme or 1 teaspoon dried thyme
1 bay leaf
2 teaspoons salt

¼ teaspoon freshly ground black pepper

3 cups half-and-half (see Cook's Notes)

¼ cup minced fresh parsley

¼ cup minced fresh cilantro (see Cook's Notes)

Fill an 8- to 10-quart stockpot two-thirds full with water, cover, and bring to a boil. (The same pot will be used to make the soup.) Prepare corn by peeling back green husks and silk. Remove from corn and discard. Cut kernels from cob by standing ear upright on a cutting board. Using a sharp knife, cut downward along cob. Discard cobs and scoop kernels into a medium mixing bowl. Add corn to boiling water and cook for 2 minutes. Drain in a colander, rinse under cold water, and let drain completely. Rinse and dry stockpot.

In a 2½-quart saucepan, place chicken breasts, celery, and 1½ cups water. Bring to a simmer over medium heat, and poach chicken just until meat turns white throughout, or an instant-read thermometer registers 160°F when inserted in thickest part of meat, about 5 minutes. Remove chicken with a slotted spoon, and set aside. Strain poaching liquid into a 4-cup glass measure, and set aside.

In the stockpot, heat vegetable oil over medium heat for about 30 seconds. Add onion and sauté for 1 minute, then cover and cook for 5 minutes longer. (Lower heat if onion is browning.) Add curry powder and cook, stirring constantly, for 2 minutes. To reserved poaching liquid, add enough stock or broth to make 2½ cups of liquid. Add this liquid along with potatoes, thyme, bay leaf, salt, and pepper to onion mixture. Raise heat to medium high and cook soup until it begins to boil. Adjust heat so soup just simmers, and cook, covered, until potatoes are tender, 15 to 20 minutes.

Add half-and-half to soup and bring to a simmer. Cut chicken into ½-inch cubes. Add chicken, reserved corn or frozen corn, parsley, and cilantro and heat through. Ladle soup into warmed individual bowls or mugs.

Cook's Notes

~< *To reduce fat, substitute 2 percent milk for the half-and-half, or use 1½ cups milk and 1½ cups half-and-half.*

~< *Cilantro is an herb you either love or hate. If you don't like the flavor, use a total of ½ cup minced fresh parsley.*

Chicken Stock

MAKES 3 TO 6 QUARTS

START TODAY to develop a very smart habit: Store necks, tails, wing tips, gizzards, hearts, backs, rib (breast) bones–anything except livers–in a gallon-size lock-top freezer bag in your freezer. When the bag is really full, you have enough chicken parts to make a small pot of homemade stock. Squeeze excess air out of the bag each time you add chicken pieces; this helps to prevent dehydration known as freezer burn. There are several time-honored methods of making chicken stock. Here is our simple approach to a basic stock.

    4 quarts (about 4 pounds) chicken parts
    1 medium unpeeled carrot
    1 medium unpeeled yellow onion
    ½ rib celery, with leaves
    ½ teaspoon whole black peppercorns
    1 bay leaf
    1 cup loosely packed parsley leaves and stems

Select a heavy 4-quart saucepan or a 6- to 8-quart stockpot. Fill it almost to the top with raw chicken parts and cover with cold water, leaving 2 inches of space at top of saucepan or stockpot. Bring to a boil over medium-high heat and reduce heat so that the liquid simmers steadily. Skim off the brown foam that rises to the top, using a soup skimmer, small tea strainer, or serving spoon. After 5 minutes or so the foam will become white; no more skimming is necessary.

Add remaining ingredients. Cover pot loosely and adjust heat so that the liquid just barely simmers. Simmer stock for 4 to 8 hours, adding water if necessary to keep the bones covered.

Remove bones and meat, draining them thoroughly in a colander or strainer set over a large bowl to catch all the juices. Discard bones and meat and pour the collected drippings into the saucepan or stockpot. Pour the stock through a fine strainer into the large bowl, then back into the pot. Set the pot into a sink filled with cold water, changing water after 10 minutes and again after 20 minutes. Cover and refrigerate for up to 3 days.

Before using the stock, scrape the congealed fat from the surface using a slotted spoon or a large serving spoon. Stock is ready to use. It can be frozen in a container, allowing 1-inch of headspace, for up to 6 months. If the stock is needed immediately after it is made, use a gravy strainer or a wide, shallow spoon (held just under the surface) to remove the liquid fat.

Winter Squash Soup

SERVES 12

HARD-SHELLED WINTER squashes such as Hubbard or Danish, and their several cousins, have many fans, including us. Their flesh is naturally sweet and richly flavored. In this soup, squash is cooked with bacon, potatoes, and chicken broth before being puréed. Small uncooked chunks of squash and potatoes are reserved and added to the soup not long before serving to contribute textural appeal.

4 slices bacon, cut crosswise into thin strips
(see Cook's Notes)

1 medium to large carrot (4 to 6 ounces),
coarsely chopped

1 rib celery, coarsely chopped

1 large yellow onion (10 to 12 ounces), peeled
and coarsely chopped

1 large red bell pepper, seeded, deveined,
and coarsely chopped

2½ to 3 pounds winter squash, such as
Hubbard, Danish, Acorn, or pumpkin

2 to 3 russet potatoes (1½ pounds), peeled
and cut into ½-inch dice

4 cups Chicken Stock (page 46) or 2 cans
(16 ounces each) low-sodium chicken broth

2 tablespoons tomato paste

1½ teaspoons dried oregano

1 teaspoon mild paprika

Freshly ground black pepper, to taste

Salt, to taste

¼ cup minced fresh parsley, for garnish

In a heavy 5-quart or larger pan, cook bacon over medium heat, stirring occasionally, until it begins to brown and renders some of its fat. Add carrot, celery, onion, and bell pepper. Cook, stirring occasionally, until vegetables are softened but not browned, 5 to 10 minutes.

Peel squash with a vegetable peeler. Cut off top of any whole squashes and set aside, and use a large serving spoon to scrape out seeds. Cut enough squash (including tops) into ½-inch pieces to equal 2 cups and set aside. Cut remaining squash in 1-inch pieces, and add to pan. Add two-thirds of potatoes to pan. Place remaining potatoes in a bowl of cold water and set aside. Add stock or broth, tomato paste, oregano, paprika, and a few grinds of pepper.

Bring soup to a boil over medium-high heat, reduce heat to simmer, cover, and cook 20 minutes. Purée soup in a blender or in food processor fitted with the metal blade, and return to pan. Taste for salt and pepper and adjust seasonings if desired. Ten minutes before serving, add reserved squash and potato pieces and simmer, covered, until they are just cooked but not mushy. Ladle soup into warmed individual bowls or mugs and garnish with parsley.

COOK'S NOTES

Cooks desiring a vegetarian soup may substitute 3 tablespoons olive oil for cooking the carrot, celery, onion, and pepper, and substitute vegetable broth for chicken broth. The smoky flavor of bacon will be lost, but the soup will still have an appealing flavor.

*

Irish Soda Bread

MAKES 1 LOAF

SODA BREADS are a great boon to the beginning cook. They are easy to make and require no specialized equipment—and they impress guests! This version can be assembled and baked in little over an hour.

1½ cups all-purpose flour, plus more for
    kneading
½ cup whole-wheat flour
½ teaspoon salt
2 teaspoons baking powder
2 teaspoons baking soda
1½ tablespoons granulated sugar
3 tablespoons unsalted butter, cold, cut into small
    cubes, plus more for coating baking sheet
1 tablespoon caraway seeds
⅓ cup currants or raisins (see Cook's Notes)
1 cup buttermilk
2 tablespoons milk

Preheat oven to 375°F. Butter a baking sheet, and set aside. In a large mixing bowl, combine dry ingredients. Stir well to blend. Scatter butter cubes over top. Using a pastry blender or your fingertips, blend butter into flour until butter is the size of tiny peas. Add caraway seeds and currants or raisins, and blend in, making sure currants or raisins are separated. Pour buttermilk over flour mixture. Blend buttermilk into flour to form a dough. As dough pulls away from side of bowl, add 1 to 2 tablespoons of flour, pat some flour onto your hands, and keeping dough in bowl, knead for 1 minute. Add a little more flour, if necessary, but dough should remain fairly sticky. Pat dough together to form a ball, then turn out onto center of prepared baking sheet. Shape bread into a coarse and bumpy-looking, 7-inch round 1 to 1½ inches thick. Use a sharp knife to cut a large X about ¼ inch deep across top of bread. Brush top with milk.

Bake until bread is nicely browned, 30 to 40 minutes. Remove to a wire rack to cool. When ready to serve, cut into wedges or slices, and place in a basket.

COOK'S NOTES

➤ *Currants can sometimes be found in supermarkets, but more often they are found in natural-food stores. Buy currants when you see them and store in a tightly sealed plastic bag in the freezer, so you'll have them on hand for baking.*

➤ *Either make this bread the day you are planning to serve it, or bake and freeze it. The bread can be baked, wrapped in plastic then in foil, and frozen for 1 month. Thaw 4 to 6 hours ahead. Warm in a preheated 400°F oven for 20 minutes prior to serving.*

Fresh Fruit
and Cheese Platter

SERVES 12

HERE IS AN ELEGANT and delicious way to end a meal–the ripest fruits of the season combined with excellent cheeses. Because this Soup and Bread Supper lends itself to fall and winter entertaining, we are recommending the fruits of these seasons. We like to offer two or three cheeses on a cheese platter. Take our suggestions as just that. Feel free to vary the fruits according to season and the cheeses according to tastes, being sure all is of the highest quality.

> ½ pound sharp Cheddar cheese, such as
>   Black Diamond or Tillamook
> ½ pound good-quality blue cheese, such as Oregon
>   blue, Danish blue, Stilton, or Roquefort
> ½ pound good-quality soft or semisoft cheese,
>   such as Taleggio or Teleme
> 2 or 3 ripe pears, preferably Comice
> 1 pound red or green grapes
> 12 ripe figs
> 2 crisp apples, such as Gala, Granny Smith, or Fuji
> 3 tangerines

Remove all cheeses from refrigerator 2 to 3 hours before serving. (Cheese is much more flavorful when not ice-cold.) Rinse all fruits, except tangerines, in a colander. Peel tangerines and section.

Use a large serving board or platter (marble is wonderful) to attractively arrange cheeses and fruits.

Provide several sharp paring knives for cutting pears, apples, and hard cheeses. Provide butter-style knives for cutting soft cheese. Offer small plates so guests can help themselves to a selection of fruit and cheese.

Sports Buffet

SERVES 12

✳ ✳ ✳

ROASTED TOMATO SALSA WITH
TORTILLA CHIPS

CARAMELIZED ONION–
SOUR CREAM DIP WITH
CARROT AND CELERY STICKS

PORTLAND CHICKEN WINGS

GREAT CHILI
(not pictured)

CHEESE QUESADILLAS

MONSTER CHOCOLATE
CHUNK COOKIES

✳

Suggested wines:

WHAT DO YOU THINK?
BEER, BEER, BEER!

Other beverages:

COFFEE, TEA

- 2 weeks in advance, make and freeze chili.

- 1 week in advance, make and freeze cookies.

- 1 day in advance, make and refrigerate onion–sour cream dip. Marinate chicken wings.

- The morning of the game, make salsa. Cut and refrigerate celery and carrots. Prepare and refrigerate ingredients for quesadillas. Thaw cookies.

- 1 hour before game time, bake chicken wings. Set out salsa, chips, onion dip, and vegetables. Warm chili.

- Halftime, make quesadillas while everyone stands around (these are so good straight out of the skillet).

- Game over–haul out that big plate of cookies.

OK GUYS, who is going to cook for Super Bowl Sunday? Go for it–you now have a game plan. Remember, read recipes ahead, plan ahead, and shop ahead. The only ones with headaches and jitters should be the coaches and players. Our menu is simple and tasty. Two highly seasoned dips satisfy the munchers, and chili, chicken wings, and quesadillas hot off the griddle will surely be devoured at halftime. Save those monster cookies for the bitter end when your crowd is cheering or lamenting their loss. Chocolate always helps!

There is no need for serving pieces galore. Serve the chili from the pot. Have a large plate to hold the chicken wings and another for the quesadillas. Have a stack of plates and bowls for the chicken and chili, and, of course, soup spoons. Remember to put out lots of napkins because everything else is finger food.

❋

Roasted Tomato Salsa with Tortilla Chips

SERVES 12

THIS IS A SIMPLE, zippy, red salsa with a good amount of heat. Feel free to adjust the heat level to your taste. It is great with chips to start the party, and is also a wonderful accompaniment to the quesadillas.

- 1½ pounds small ripe tomatoes (4 to 8), split in half horizontally and seeded (see Cook's Notes)
- 3 fresh serrano chilies, split lengthwise, seeded, and finely chopped (see Cook's Notes)
- 1 medium red onion (about 8 ounces), peeled and chopped
- 1 tablespoon rice wine vinegar (see Cook's Notes)
- ¼ teaspoon granulated sugar
- ½ cup chopped fresh cilantro
- 1 fresh jalapeño chile, split lengthwise, seeded, and thinly sliced, for garnish (optional)
- 1 large bag tortilla chips

Preheat broiler. Place tomato halves, cut sides down, on a nonstick baking sheet or a baking sheet lined with aluminum foil to make cleanup easier. Broil until skin of tomatoes has blistered and blackened. Let cool on paper towels to absorb excess moisture. Coarsely chop and place in a medium mixing bowl with serrano chilies, red onion, vinegar, sugar, and cilantro. When ready to serve, transfer to serving dish and garnish with sliced jalapeño, if using. Serve with tortilla chips.

~ *Much of the year, the best choice for tomatoes for this salsa will be Roma, or plum, tomatoes. However, some excellent hydroponic tomatoes are available all year. Choose whichever tomato is the brightest red (anemic pink ones shouldn't even be called tomatoes!).*

~ *Serrano chilies are smaller and hotter than jalapeño chilies. If you cannot find serranos, jalapeños are fine. We suggest 4 or 5 of them, split and seeded.*

~ *We recommend rice wine vinegar, but plain, white distilled vinegar can be substituted.*

~ *This salsa is best served the day it is made. However, it can be made 1 day in advance with a little loss of freshness.*

❋

Caramelized Onion– Sour Cream Dip with Carrot and Celery Sticks

SERVES 10

Based on sour cream (the real thing, not the low-fat or nonfat variety) and caramelized onions, perfumed with curry powder, and flecked with toasted sesame seeds, this dip is very easy to prepare and was quite a hit when presented to our panel of professional couch potatoes. You need only a heavy-bottomed frying pan to caramelize the onions, a technique frequently used in Indian cooking.

2 tablespoons raw sesame seeds

1 tablespoon curry powder

1 tablespoon vegetable oil

2 large yellow onions (about 1 pound total), peeled and coarsely chopped

2 cups (16 ounces) sour cream

A few tablespoons buttermilk

5 medium carrots

5 ribs celery

In a heavy-bottomed 10- to 12-inch frying pan over medium-low heat, toast sesame seeds until they turn light brown, about 5 minutes. Remove from heat as soon as they are toasted, so they do not burn. Set aside. Toast curry powder in the same manner until it is fragrant, 1 to 2 minutes. Set aside.

Raise heat to medium-high, and add oil and onions. Cook, stirring frequently, until onions are very brown–almost black–but have not charred. They should taste a little sweet, not bitter. Depending on heat level, size of pan, and water content of onions, caramelizing can take 20 to 40 minutes. Scrape onions onto a wide plate to cool a few minutes. In a medium mixing bowl, stir sour cream to loosen its texture. Add reserved sesame seeds, curry powder, and cooked onions. Stir to blend. Cover and refrigerate until serving. Thin, if necessary, at serving time with a little buttermilk.

Cut carrots into 3-inch lengths, then cut lengthwise into quarters. Using a vegetable peeler, lightly peel back of celery ribs to remove strings. Cut ribs into 3-inch lengths, then cut in half lengthwise. Arrange carrots and celery on a serving platter, cover with damp paper towels, then with plastic wrap, and refrigerate until serving time.

Caramelizing onions in a frying pan without a non-stick coating usually leaves a burned-looking residue in the pan. To facilitate cleanup, fill the pan with water, bring to a boil, then soak several hours or overnight.

✳

Portland Chicken Wings

SERVES 12

BUFFALO LANDED on the food map first for its chicken wings. Now it's Portland's turn. It's just a matter of time before these delectable wings appear on bar menus. We thought we better make plenty for a hungry crowd. If your crowd is smaller, enjoy the leftovers. This is great finger food. Serve with plenty of napkins.

3½ to 4 pounds chicken wings or chicken wing
    drumettes (see Cook's Notes)

Marinade
1 tablespoon dry mustard
1 teaspoon paprika
2 tablespoons rice wine vinegar
1 tablespoon Tabasco sauce
2 tablespoons Worcestershire sauce
¼ cup low-sodium soy sauce
½ cup honey

Cut wing tips at joint and remove from chicken wings. (Reserve these separately for making stock. See page 46.) Place chicken wings in a large, heavy-duty lock-top plastic bag.

To make marinade, in a 1-cup glass measure mix mustard, paprika, and vinegar to form a smooth paste.

Add Tabasco, Worcestershire, and soy sauce, and stir to combine. Add honey and mix well. Pour over chicken wings, seal bag, and tilt bag to distribute marinade. Set bag on its side in a 9-by-13-inch baking dish (just in case bag leaks). Refrigerate at least 2 hours, or up to 24 hours, turning occasionally.

Preheat oven to 450°F. Prepare 2 rimmed baking sheets by lining bottom and sides with foil. (This saves messy cleanup.) Remove chicken wings from marinade and place in a single layer on prepared baking sheets. Space wings 1 inch apart so they cook evenly. Bake 15 minutes. Brush chicken with a little marinade, and rotate pans. Lower oven temperature to 350°F and bake 20 minutes longer. If chicken looks dry or is browning too much, brush with a bit more marinade during last 20 minutes of cooking. Place on a warmed platter and serve.

A short course in Chicken Anatomy 101. There are 3 parts to a chicken wing: the wing tip, the center section with 2 bones, and the drumette which looks like a miniature drumstick. Buying just the drumettes is preferable because they are the meatiest parts. On occasion, you'll see drumettes in supermarkets, but if you plan in advance, a butcher can order them for you.

It feels like a bonus to save the wing tips for stock. Freeze in a heavy-duty lock-top freezer bag and save for making stock.

Portland Chicken Wings reheat well in a preheated 350°F oven or in a microwave. They aren't quite as crisp after being refrigerated, but the taste is still great.

❋
Great Chili

SERVES 10 TO 12

IN OUR EARLIER BOOK, *The Basic Gourmet,* we offer a very good recipe for a three-bean meatless chili, along with a variation using added ground beef. This chili con carne–literally, a chili-flavored soup with added meat–uses somewhat different seasonings and coarsely ground beef often labeled "chili grind." It is a straightforward, bold, rich bowl of red that you can heat up by adding more crushed dried red pepper (really crushed dried red chilies). It relies more on the beef and less on the beans than our other version, so folks with bull on their boots might find it more traditional. Some chiliheads swear that adding beans to chili con carne is a hanging offense, so add the beans at your own risk!

2 pounds very coarsely ground beef chuck or
　　lean beef (see Cook's Notes)
2 tablespoons vegetable oil (optional)
2 large yellow onions (about 12 ounces each),
　　peeled and coarsely chopped
4 large cloves garlic, peeled and coarsely chopped
3 tablespoons chili con carne seasoning (see
　　Cook's Notes)
1 teaspoon ground cinnamon
1 teaspoon ground cumin
½ teaspoon crushed dried red pepper, plus
　　more to taste
1 bay leaf
1 teaspoon dried oregano
½ teaspoon dried thyme
1 teaspoon salt, plus more to taste
1 teaspoon sugar
1 bottle (12 ounces) beer (plus optional bottle
　　for the cook)
1 can (16 ounces) beef broth
1 can (28 ounces) peeled, chopped tomatoes
　　with liquid
1 can (15 ounces) pinto beans (optional)
Cornmeal, for thickening chili (optional)

In a 4-quart or larger saucepan or sauté pan over medium-high heat, brown beef. With a slotted spoon, remove beef from pan and set aside on a paper towel-lined plate to drain. Pour off all but 2 tablespoons of any beef fat in pan or add vegetable oil as necessary to make a total of 2 tablespoons fat. Add onions and garlic, and sauté over medium heat, stirring occasionally, until vegetables are soft but not browned, about 10 minutes. Add chili con carne seasoning, cinnamon, cumin, red pepper, bay leaf, oregano, thyme, salt, and sugar. Stir into onions and cook for 1 to 2 minutes. Add beer, broth, and tomatoes. Bring to a boil, reduce heat to simmer, cover, and cook 1 hour.

Taste for seasoning, and add more salt or red pepper if desired. Add beans, if using. Thicken, if desired, by stirring in cornmeal, 1 tablespoon at a time, and cooking for 3 minutes after each addition.

COOK'S NOTES

➤ *Pork or lamb also tastes terrific in chili con carne.*

➤ *The chili can be frozen for up to 3 months stored in tightly covered plastic containers or large lock-top plastic bags. It can also be refrigerated for 5 days. Thaw frozen chili in refrigerator for 2 days or use defrost setting on a microwave oven. The optional cornmeal thickening should be added after chili has been rewarmed, a few minutes before serving.*

~ *Chili con carne seasoning (rather than chili powder) is a commercial blend of red chile peppers, spices, and garlic intended for exactly this kind of recipe. You may experiment with chili powder, or ground mild red chilies and your favorite dried herbs to create your own seasoning blend, if you prefer.*

❋

Cheese Quesadillas

SERVES 12

QUESADILLAS ARE the Mexican version of grilled cheese sandwiches. All you need to make them are flour tortillas and thinly sliced or grated cheese, and the condiments of your choice. For a buffet, cut the quesadillas into six wedges using a sharp knife or pizza cutter and arrange them on a platter. Serve with more salsa and let your guests help themselves.

12 flour tortillas, 10 inches in diameter
12 ounces pepper Jack cheese or Monterey Jack
    cheese, grated or thinly sliced
½ cup Roasted Tomato Salsa (page 52),
    for accompaniment

Condiments (optional)
4 medium tomatillos, husked, rinsed, and sliced
    into paper-thin rounds (see Cook's Notes)
½ cup fresh cilantro leaves (see Cook's Notes)
2 scallions with 4 inches of green part, minced

Heat 1 or 2 heavy-bottomed, 10-inch frying pans over high heat until hot. (Using 2 pans allows you to make 2 quesadillas at once.) Place a tortilla in each pan, and sprinkle with ½ cup grated cheese or cover with 5 or 6 slices. When cheese begins to melt, add 2 tablespoons of one or more of the condiments, if desired. Cover with another tortilla. When bottom tortilla is nicely browned, use a spatula to turn quesadilla. Brown other side. Place on a cutting board, and use a sharp knife or a pizza cutter to cut into 6 wedges. Continue until all tortillas are cooked. Arrange wedges on a platter and serve while warm and crisp. Have a small bowl of the salsa next to platter so guests can spoon a little salsa on top of quesadillas, if desired.

COOK'S NOTES

~ *Tomatillos, which look like small, green tomatoes with an outer papery husk, add a tart, fresh taste to quesadillas. They are readily available in the produce section of well-stocked supermarkets.*

~ *We love the taste of fresh cilantro (also known as fresh coriander) and think it tastes great with the pepper Jack cheese. Not everyone agrees, so we suggest making some of the quesadillas without it.*

~ *Vary the cheeses to suit your taste. Use Cheddar, Muenster, Provolone, or a combination.*

Monster Chocolate Chunk Cookies

MAKES 20 COOKIES

THESE ARE A COOKIE lover's dream! Filled with big chunks of chocolate and walnuts, they are a real "handful" of cookie. Although you can use chocolate chips, it is the big chocolate chunks that make these special. Buy the best semisweet chocolate you can find, such as Callebaut, Guittard, Ghirardelli, or Valrhona, because the flavor will come through in every delicious mouthful.

12 ounces good-quality semisweet chocolate

1 ½ sticks (6 ounces) unsalted butter, softened

¾ cup brown sugar, firmly packed

2 large eggs

1½ teaspoons pure vanilla extract

2 cups all-purpose flour

½ teaspoon baking powder

¼ teaspoon salt

8 ounces walnuts, very coarsely chopped

Preheat oven to 350°F. Line 2 baking sheets with aluminum foil or use nonstick baking sheets.

Break up chocolate into ¼- to ½-inch chunks. This is best done on a cutting board with a carving fork. Set aside.

In a large mixing bowl, cream butter and brown sugar with an electric mixer or by hand until fluffy. Add eggs, 1 at a time, beating well after each addition. Add vanilla and blend. Add flour, baking powder, and salt, and mix until just incorporated. Add walnuts and reserved chocolate, and stir to blend with a large spatula. Dough will be quite stiff.

For each cookie, generously fill a ¼-cup measure with dough. Place portions of dough 1½-inches apart on baking sheets. Bake until firm to the touch and lightly brown, 18 to 20 minutes. Allow to set on baking sheets for 2 to 3 minutes before removing to wire racks to cool completely. Arrange on a serving plate.

COOK'S NOTES

➤ *The cookies will keep at room temperature, well wrapped, for 4 to 5 days. They can be frozen for 1 month. Layer between sheets of waxed paper in lock-top plastic bags.*

CHAPTER 3

Sit-down Dinners

✳   ✳   ✳

Three-Course Dinner

Three-Course Dinner in an Hour

Four-Course Dinner

Another Four-Course Dinner

✳

*P*ERHAPS THE GREATEST compliment you can pay family, friends, and colleagues is to invite them to sit down to your table and partake of your food. The bonds developed around the table transcend culture, class, and generation. The world would be a better place if we dined together more often, a thought all too frequently lost in the drive-up line at the local fast-food joint.

Your food does not have to be fancy when you invite someone to your home. In fact, the most successful meals are those where the hosts are relaxed. Trying to tackle a twelve-page recipe from the newest guru of designer cooking can be frustrating and exhausting. You will have more fun when you cook what looks appealing to you and is within your skill range (we're here to help).

We have divided our sit-down dinners into graduated levels of complexity and formality. In all cases we've given you do-ahead tips. Since you want to spend time with your guests, we encourage you to prepare as much as possible in advance. Our first Three-Course Dinner is one of the warmest, simplest, and most satisfying you can find. A simple salad, a braised chicken, and a big piece of homemade apple pie make you the hero of the moment. Simple china, flowers on the table, and a pleasant wine are all you need to complete the setting.

The same can be said for the Three-Course Dinner in an Hour. This is not a joke: It can be done in an hour, and it is wonderful. A very quick sauté of chicken breast is accompanied by a simple aromatic herbed rice dish. The dessert is delicious and can nearly be done with your eyes closed.

Our two four-course dinners raise the level of sophistication a bit. The first dinner celebrates the popular Asian influence in our food with an Asian noodle salad, mushroom soup, and grilled pork. The second is elegant but easy, and can be pulled out when you want a special-occasion meal. We add an Italian touch by offering pasta as a first-course, then following it with whole roasted Cornish game hens and a delightful apple cake.

You can modify the menus to suit your or your guests' preferences or to accommodate the preparation time you have available. If you are unable or don't want to make dessert, buy some good ice cream and cookies. High-quality prepared foods from better supermarkets and specialty stores can be used to augment various courses of your meal. Remember, if you cook what you can, generously and graciously, you are giving your guests one of the greatest gifts possible.

Three-Course Dinner

SERVES 6

❋ ❋ ❋

ICEBERG LETTUCE WITH
BLUE CHEESE DRESSING
(not pictured)

CHICKEN PAPRIKASH
AND BUTTERED NOODLES

DAN'S APPLE PIE

❋

Suggested wine:
DRY RIESLING OR TOKAY

❋

- 2 to 3 days in advance, make and refrigerate salad dressing. Prepare and cook chicken.

- 1 day in advance, make and refrigerate pie dough.

- The morning of serving, make pie filling, roll out pie dough, and assemble and bake pie.

- About 1 hour before serving, reheat chicken. Cook noodles and keep warm. Cut lettuce and chop parsley for garnish.

- Just before serving, assemble salads.

- When serving entrée, put ice cream in refrigerator to soften, if using to accompany pie.

THIS MENU IS DESIGNED for simple, homey entertaining. Nothing fancy, just some true-blue flavors that everyone loves. The first course is straight from the heartland. Food snobs can pooh-pooh iceberg lettuce and opt only for organic baby greens, but do you know what? This salad is pretty darn good. Cold, crisp lettuce with a creamy, assertive dressing makes just the right start to this meal. Chicken Paprikash with Buttered Noodles is the food of our grandmothers. The chicken is braised on the stove top, so the wonderful aroma of onions and sweet paprika fills your home. This entrée could be served family style or on individual plates. When the chicken is served on a platter, guests can choose the parts they like best. Because there is a generous amount of sauce, you have the option of serving some separately in a sauceboat or little pitcher. Homemade apple pie with a small scoop of ice cream makes a satisfying end to a comforting meal.

If you are serving family style, warm a platter for the chicken and a bowl for the noodles, and have the dinner plates already stacked on the table. If you are planning to serve individual entrées, the dinner plates should be warm and kept in the kitchen. For each diner, you'll need a plate for the salad course and for dessert. Set the table with a knife, a spoon, and three forks if you have them; otherwise, wash the salad forks to use for dessert. Set a water glass and a wineglass. Flowers and candles are always nice, but this menu really lends itself to simplicity.

✳

Iceberg Lettuce with Blue Cheese Dressing

SERVES 6

BACK IN THE 1950s and 1960s, wedges of iceberg lettuce with blue cheese dressing could be found in the cafeterias and lunchrooms of Middle America. They are back in style for good reason—they're great. The better the blue cheese, the better the dressing. Our recommendations are Danish blue, Oregon blue, Maytag blue, and, of course, glorious Roquefort.

1 head iceberg lettuce (about 1½ pounds)

Dressing
¾ cup mayonnaise
¾ cup plain low-fat yogurt
1 cup crumbled blue cheese (about 6 ounces)
¼ cup chopped fresh parsley
2 to 2½ tablespoons freshly squeezed
    lemon juice (about 1 lemon)
Salt and freshly ground black pepper, to taste

Trim outer leaves from head of iceberg, and discard. Remove core and cut head into 6 wedges. Do not wash lettuce, which will make dressing watery. Place each wedge on a salad plate, cut side down, and refrigerate.

To make dressing, in a medium mixing bowl, combine mayonnaise, yogurt, ⅔ cup of the blue cheese, and half of the chopped parsley. Add 2 tablespoons lemon juice, and stir to blend. Taste and add more lemon juice if desired. Season to taste with salt and pepper.

Spoon dressing over lettuce wedges. Garnish with the remaining ⅓ cup blue cheese and chopped parsley, divided among wedges. Serve immediately.

❋

Chicken Paprikash and Buttered Noodles

SERVES 6

THIS ENTRÉE IS an old family favorite. Friday night supper was either brisket or chicken, and Chicken Paprikash was one of the memorable meals. This recipe was created from taste memories and the cooking techniques refined from experience because, frankly, in the kitchen of our youth there wasn't an instant-read thermometer in sight! Any written family recipe for this dish would have said something like, "cook for two hours or all day." We recommend using chicken breasts and thighs. If you prefer all white meat or all dark meat, select your favorite parts. Keep in mind that you need a total of 3¾ to 4 pounds of chicken.

Chicken

½ cup all-purpose flour

5 tablespoons Hungarian sweet paprika, divided (see Cook's Notes)

1½ teaspoons salt

½ teaspoon freshly ground black pepper

4 chicken breast halves, bone in, with skin (see Cook's Notes)

4 chicken thighs

¼ cup vegetable oil

1 large yellow onion (about 12 ounces), peeled and cut into ½-inch dice

1 large fresh tomato (about 8 ounces), peeled, seeded, and diced (see Cook's Notes)

1 large green bell pepper (about 8 ounces), seeded, deveined, and cut into ½-inch dice

2 tablespoons sour cream

¼ cup minced fresh parsley

Noodles

2 teaspoons salt

1 package (16 ounces) extra-wide egg noodles or dumpling egg noodles

3 tablespoons unsalted butter, melted

¼ cup minced fresh parsley

To make chicken, in a large, heavy-duty plastic bag, mix flour with 3 tablespoons of the paprika, salt, and pepper. Add chicken, and close tightly. Shake well to coat chicken parts.

In a straight-sided, 12-inch frying pan over medium-high heat, heat oil. Place chicken in a single layer in pan and brown on both sides, about 5 minutes per side. Remove to a large plate. Add onion and sauté until translucent, about 5 minutes. Add the remaining 2 tablespoons paprika and sauté 2 minutes longer. Return chicken to pan and add diced tomato and 1½ cups water. Bring to a simmer, turn heat to low, cover, and cook for 20 minutes. Add bell pepper and cook 15 minutes longer. Chicken is done when an instant-read thermometer inserted into center of breast meat or thigh registers 170°F. Using a slotted spoon, remove chicken to a warm serving platter. Stir sour cream and parsley into liquid in pan, then spoon over chicken.

To cook noodles, fill an 8-quart stockpot three-quarters full with water, cover, and bring to a boil over high heat. Add salt, then add noodles. Cook until al dente with a little bite remaining; check package directions for suggested cooking time. Noodles shouldn't be mushy. Stir noodles several times to prevent them from sticking to bottom of pan. Drain, but do not rinse. Place in a large serving bowl, add butter and parsley, and toss to mix. Serve immediately, or cover tightly with foil and keep warm, up to 1 hour, in a 200°F oven.

Cook's Notes
In highly specialized markets, you might find as many as six different styles of Hungarian paprika, but generally, the two most common types are "sweet" and "hot." You want Hungarian sweet paprika for this dish, but add some hot paprika if you want to spice it up.

Remove peel from tomatoes by blanching in boiling water for 15 to 30 seconds before slipping skins off. Or use a sharp, swivel-action vegetable peeler to remove skin.

This is a great do-ahead dish. Make it up to 3 days before you plan to serve it and refrigerate until 1 hour before serving. Don't add sour cream and parsley until you reheat on top of stove or in a preheated 350°F oven.

<hr>

Dan's Apple Pie
MAKES ONE 10-INCH PIE

ROLLING OUT a little pie dough builds character, and besides, it qualifies the cook for a larger-than-average piece of the pie! Your guests are going to want to hug you when they taste this. It's especially appealing served with top-quality vanilla ice cream.

Crust
2½ cups all-purpose flour, plus flour for dusting
1 teaspoon salt
2 tablespoons granulated sugar
11 tablespoons unsalted butter, very cold
7 tablespoons solid vegetable shortening, very cold
⅓ cup very cold water, plus more as needed
2 tablespoons whipping cream

Filling
About 8 crisp, tart apples (2½ to 3 pounds) such as Granny Smith or Pippin
Zest of 1 lemon, minced, plus 2 tablespoons juice
½ cup granulated sugar
½ cup gently packed brown sugar
¼ teaspoon ground nutmeg
1 teaspoon ground cinnamon
½ teaspoon salt

½ cup walnut pieces

3 tablespoons quick-cooking tapioca

2 tablespoons unsalted butter

1 pint vanilla ice cream (optional)

To make crust, place dry ingredients in a food processor fitted with the metal blade. Cut butter and shortening into tablespoon-size pieces and place in workbowl. Use pulse button to blend until butter and shortening pieces are between size of peas and lima beans. Add the water and quickly process for a few seconds just until a ball of dough begins to form. Add 1 tablespoon water at a time if needed to form dough into a mass. Do not process after dough ball forms. Remove dough from workbowl, gathering all loose bits, and cut into 2 pieces. One piece should be larger, about two-thirds of total dough. Form each piece into a ball, flatten to about 1 inch thick, enclose in plastic wrap, and refrigerate at least 30 minutes, or as long as overnight.

Position a rack in middle to lower third of oven, and preheat oven to 400°F. Have ready a 10-inch pie pan.

To make filling, peel and core apples. Cut into slices about ¼ inch thick, or slice with a food processor fitted with an 8-millimeter slicing disc. You need about 8 cups of slices. Place apple slices in a large mixing bowl and toss with remaining ingredients except butter. Let stand while you roll out dough.

On a lightly floured work surface, roll out larger piece of dough to a circle about 13 inches in diameter. Dust work surface and dough with a little more flour if necessary to keep dough from sticking. Dough will be very delicate, and its edges do not have to be perfectly smooth. Roll up dough circle around rolling pin, lift over pie plate, and unroll dough over plate, allowing it to settle into plate. Moisten dough with a little cold water to patch any holes or cracks.

Place apple mixture in pie plate. Cut 2 tablespoons butter into pea-size pieces and sprinkle over apples.

Roll out remaining piece of dough into a circle about 12 inches in diameter. Roll dough around rolling pin as for larger circle, transfer to pie pan, and cover apple mixture. Use your thumbs or a fork to press dough layers together around rim of pie pan, then use a knife to trim off excess dough around pan. Cut 4 or 5 small slits in top crust so steam can escape during baking. Brush whipping cream evenly over top of pie and place pie in oven on a baking sheet or large piece of aluminum foil to catch drips.

Bake for 20 minutes. Reduce heat to 350°F, and bake until top crust is golden brown, about 40 minutes longer. Cool on a wire rack for at least 1 hour before cutting into wedges and serving. Accompany each serving with a scoop of vanilla ice cream, if desired.

COOK'S NOTES

Pie is also wonderful topped with a slice of high-quality Cheddar such as Canadian Black Diamond or Tillamook Reserve.

Three-Course Dinner in an Hour

SERVES 6

❋ ❋ ❋

SPINACH SALAD WITH MUSHROOMS
AND SWEET RED PEPPERS

SAUTÉED CHICKEN BREASTS WITH
TARRAGON AND LIME

HERBED RICE WITH CELERY

ICE CREAM WITH BANANAS,
RUM, AND CREAM
(not pictured)

❋

Suggested wine:
SAUVIGNON BLANC

❋

- 1 hour in advance, make rice. Prepare ingredients for spinach salad and make vinaigrette. Cut lime garnish for chicken, and prepare chicken for cooking.

- Toss and serve salad, then sauté and serve chicken and rice.

- When serving entrée, transfer ice cream from freezer to refrigerator.

- Prepare dessert and coffee after entrée.

YOU DON'T NEED to strap on Rollerblades or put on your sweatband to prepare this meal. You just need to be organized! With our planning-ahead guide, we truly believe the beginning cook can make this meal in an hour. Let your guests sip wine and enjoy each other's company while you put the finishing touches on the meal. This is a meal where the table is set simply—napkin, wineglass, knife, two forks, and spoon for each guest.

There is no sacrificing of taste for time in this menu. The spinach salad has a lively mustard vinaigrette that complements the mushrooms, red onion, and sweet red pepper. Crisply coated chicken breasts are highlighted by tarragon and tangy lime, while the rice nicely completes the plate. Your friends will be screaming for more ice cream when they taste this combination of bananas, rum, and cream. Bring on a pot of decaf to serve with dessert.

Our timesaving tips—such as buying prewashed spinach, having the chicken be the last item placed on the cutting board (which saves extra washing), and refrigerating ice cream 20 minutes prior to serving it—keeps you focused. If you feel quite at ease at the stove, use two frying pans to sauté the chicken instead of frying two batches. You can decide between an extra pan to clean up or a quicker sautéing time. There are always trade-offs!

❋

Spinach Salad with Mushrooms and Sweet Red Peppers

SERVES 6

THIS SALAD PARTNERS well with the chicken sauté and can be served before, after, or at the same time as the main course. Many supermarkets sell prewashed and trimmed spinach in plastic bags. The greens usually don't need washing and stay fresh for several days in the refrigerator. Refer to the dressing as a "Dijon vinaigrette" rather than "vinegar, oil, and mustard dressing" if you need to impress someone!

Salad
2 bunches spinach (about 10 ounces each)
8 ounces white or brown mushrooms
¼ large red bell pepper (1 to 2 ounces), seeded and deveined
Small piece red onion (1 to 2 ounces)

Dressing
¼ cup extra-virgin olive oil
1 tablespoon red wine vinegar
1 tablespoon Dijon-style mustard
½ teaspoon granulated sugar
Scant ½ teaspoon salt, plus more to taste
Freshly ground black pepper, to taste

Trim spinach by cutting off bunch of stems just behind leaves. Some leaves will still have short stems. If your life seems too simple, remove them; we think they taste fine and add crunchy texture. Fill a clean sink or very large bowl with cool water, toss in spinach, and agitate with your hands to encourage dirt and sand to fall to bottom of sink or bowl. Transfer spinach to a colander, then drain sink or bowl to remove grit. Repeat. Dry spinach in a salad spinner or with paper towels, and refrigerate in a plastic bag until serving time. Brush mushrooms with a bit of paper towel or a soft mushroom brush, and trim stem ends if they are dark. Cut each mushroom through stem into quarters if small, or into 6 to 8 pieces if large, and set aside. Thinly slice bell peppers, and set aside. Thinly slice onion, and set aside.

To make dressing, in a small jar with a tight-fitting lid, combine olive oil, vinegar, mustard, sugar, salt, and pepper. Cover tightly and shake vigorously to blend ingredients.

When ready to serve, place spinach, mushrooms, pepper, and onion in a large serving bowl. Give dressing a last-minute shake and pour over salad. Toss, taste for seasoning, and add more salt or pepper, if desired. Serve at once on individual salad plates.

※

Sautéed Chicken Breasts with Tarragon and Lime

SERVES 6

THIS RECIPE has become a regular in our cooking repertoire. Using three coatings for the chicken is a classic technique. By dipping the chicken breasts first in flour, the egg has something to hold on to. The egg coating provides additional moisture and flavor and holds the bread crumbs, which offer a crusty texture. If you get organized at the outset by assembling two baking sheets, two plates for the flour and bread crumbs, and a bowl for the eggs, then you just have to coat and sauté the chicken.

> 3 whole or 6 half boneless, skinless chicken breasts
> ⅓ cup all-purpose flour
> 3 large eggs
> 1½ cups unseasoned dry bread crumbs
> 1 teaspoon salt
> ½ teaspoon freshly ground black pepper
> ½ teaspoon granulated sugar
> ¼ cup minced fresh tarragon or 2 tablespoons dried tarragon leaves
> 2 tablespoons olive oil, plus more as needed
> 2 tablespoons unsalted butter, plus more as needed
> 2 limes, cut into wedges, for garnish

Place a long piece of plastic wrap on a work surface. Set chicken breasts, about 3 inches apart, on plastic, then cover with another piece of plastic wrap. Using a flat (nonserrated) meat pounder or bottom of a small saucepan, pound chicken so it is uniformly thin, without tearing it.

Organize the 3 coatings. Place flour on a dinner plate. In a shallow, wide bowl, beat eggs together; set next to flour. Combine bread crumbs, salt, pepper, sugar, and tarragon on another plate and set next to eggs. Have ready 2 baking sheets. Lightly coat each chicken breast first with flour, shaking off excess. Then dip in egg and let excess drain off. Finally, coat lightly but completely with crumb mixture. Place on baking sheets until ready to sauté. (This may be done up to 6 hours in advance. Cover tightly with plastic wrap and refrigerate until ready to cook.)

Heat a heavy, 12-inch frying pan (preferably cast iron) over medium-high heat, add oil and butter, and tilt to coat pan. (If sautéing chicken in 2 batches, preheat oven to 200°F.) Add chicken to pan without crowding and sauté until bread coating looks crisp and golden, 2 to 3 minutes per side. Sauté a second batch, adding additional oil and butter if needed. Keep first batch warm while sautéing second. Serve hot, garnished with lime wedges.

※

Herbed Rice with Celery

SERVES 6

DICED CELERY and chopped parsley contrast with white rice to produce a very attractive side dish. Dishes based on rice can be very easy to put together, and they take little cooking time–two reasons why rice is always on our shelf. We generally use basmati rice, but a generic long grain will do handsomely.

2 cups long-grain white rice
3¼ cups water
1 teaspoon salt
1 teaspoon celery seed
Freshly ground black pepper, to taste
2 ribs celery, finely diced
½ cup chopped fresh parsley

Place rice in a fine-mesh sieve and rinse under cold running water for a few seconds. Shake dry and place in a 3-quart or larger saucepan. Add the water. Bring to a boil over medium-high heat, reduce to a bare simmer, add salt and celery seed, and cover. Cook undisturbed for 15 minutes. Remove from heat and allow to stand 10 minutes, covered. Add pepper to taste, celery, and parsley, and stir to blend. A single chopstick stirred in one direction is an efficient way to blend seasonings into rice without compacting rice into a gluey mass. Taste for salt and add more if desired.

✳

Ice Cream with Bananas, Rum, and Cream

SERVES 6

HERE'S A NIFTY dessert that you can just about pull off with your eyes closed. You don't even have to begin to think about it until dinner is done. It takes minutes to put together while your guests are happily chatting. We've designed the recipe to serve six, but if any bananas and cream are left, they are very good for breakfast even if the bananas are a little brown.

¾ cup whipping cream
6 tablespoons dark rum
2 tablespoons sour cream
6 large, ripe bananas
1 pint vanilla ice cream
1 pint coffee ice cream

In a large mixing bowl, whisk together whipping cream, rum, and sour cream. Peel bananas and slice ½ inch thick, placing them in cream as you slice. Toss banana slices with cream mixture. It will thicken slightly.

Put one scoop each of vanilla ice cream and coffee ice cream in 6 serving bowls. Top each with a generous portion of bananas and cream. Serve at once.

Four-Course Dinner

SERVES 8

✳ ✳ ✳

ASIAN NOODLE SALAD

CREAM OF BLACK MUSHROOM SOUP
(not pictured)

HOISIN-GRILLED PORK TENDERLOIN

GRILLED ASPARAGUS

CARAMEL ICE CREAM PIE
(not pictured)

✳

Suggested wine:
PINOT NOIR

✳

- ◉ 1 to 2 weeks in advance, make and freeze pie.

- ◉ 2 days in advance, make and refrigerate soup.

- ◉ 1 day in advance, make and refrigerate salad.

- ◉ The day of serving, wash and trim asparagus and refrigerate. Trim and refrigerate pork. Prepare sauce for pork.

- ◉ About 45 minutes before serving, heat soup, bring salad to room temperature and light grill. Coat pork with sauce. Coat asparagus with oil.

- ◉ Serve noodle salad, then soup. Grill pork and asparagus and serve. Just before you sit down, transfer ice-cream pie from freezer to refrigerator.

IF YOU FIND GRILLING easy, you can prepare this menu on a weeknight after a day's work. With the noodle salad, soup, and dessert all made ahead, you can come home from work and prepare the pork and asparagus. You'll sip some wine along with your guests and ease into the evening. The noodle salad is a terrific starter. Its spicy flavors get soothed by the creaminess of the black mushroom soup that follows. Grilled pork tenderloin, smoky and sweet, will be fork tender, a nice contrast to the crisp, slightly charred asparagus. No one will pass up the winning combination of caramel and vanilla for dessert.

The strategy for this menu calls for grilling the pork and asparagus after serving the second course. Hosts sometimes feel that multiple-course meals should flow as they do in a restaurant. At home, when you have made guests feel comfortable, it doesn't matter if there is lag time between the second course and the entrée. A little wait for fresh-off-the-grill pork tenderloin and asparagus is worth it. You can grill before you sit down for the salad course, keeping the food warm in a preheated 250°F oven, but some quality is sacrificed.

About the table: You will need small plates for the noodle salad and pie, soup bowls, and entrée plates. Each place should be set with a napkin, a knife, a soup spoon, a teaspoon, and three forks–salad fork, entrée fork, and dessert fork. ("Hey, that's a lot of forks!" we hear you say; well, wash the salad forks and use them again if need be.) You could also buy chopsticks for the noodle salad.

Asian Noodle Salad

SERVES 8

ASIAN NOODLE SALADS are versatile and easy to make, and can be prepared three to four days in advance. Supermarkets generally carry several different kinds of noodles. If you can find buckwheat soba (*soba* means "noodle"), buy them. Otherwise, purchase any thin, wheat-based noodle. Avoid Asian noodles that look glassy, called "bean threads." Italian-style spaghettis are also fine. If chili oil is unavailable, use about 1 tablespoon of a liquid hot pepper sauce.

⅓ cup soy sauce (regular or low-sodium)
⅓ cup firmly packed brown sugar
½ cup Asian sesame oil
2 tablespoons Chinese chili oil
2 tablespoons red wine vinegar

4 scallions with about 1 inch of green parts,
    cut into thin rings
1 tablespoon salt
¾ pound thin, wheat-based noodles
3 sprigs fresh cilantro, for garnish (optional)
1 red bell pepper, seeded, deveined, and thinly
    sliced, for garnish (optional)

Fill a 6- to 8-quart stockpot two-thirds full of water, cover, and bring to a boil over high heat. In a 1-quart saucepan over low heat, warm soy sauce. Add brown sugar, sesame oil, chili oil, vinegar, and scallions. Stir to dissolve brown sugar. Remove from heat and set aside.

When pasta water has reached a boil, add salt and then noodles. Cook noodles until al dente (with a little bite remaining), 6 to 7 minutes. They shouldn't be mushy, but if they still have a crunchy, raw center, cook for 1 to 2 minutes longer, and taste again.

Drain noodles thoroughly in a colander. Place in a large mixing bowl and pour sauce over them. Toss well and allow noodles to cool before covering and refrigerating. Refrigerate at least 3 hours before serving.

To serve, divide noodles among 8 salad plates or bowls. Garnish with cilantro and red pepper, if desired.

❊

Cream of Black Mushroom Soup

SERVES 8

THE FLAVORS OF THIS SOUP are delicate and subtle. The creaminess balances the spiciness of the first course.

6 cups Chicken Stock (page 46) or 3 cans
    (16 ounces each) low-sodium chicken broth
12 medium fresh mushrooms wiped clean
20 dried Chinese or Japanese black mushrooms
    (see Cook's Notes)
2 ribs celery with leaves, cut into 2-inch lengths
1 medium carrot, cut into 2-inch lengths
1 medium yellow onion, peel intact and quartered
2 tablespoons unsalted butter, softened
2 tablespoons all-purpose flour
2 cups whipping cream
¼ cup port wine
Salt and freshly ground black pepper, to taste
¼ cup minced fresh parsley, for garnish

In a 4-quart saucepan, combine stock, mushrooms, celery, carrot, and onion. Bring to a boil over medium-high heat, then reduce heat so stock or broth just simmers. Cover, and cook for 30 minutes. Cool slightly.

Set a fine-mesh strainer over a bowl large enough to hold stock or broth. Carefully pour or ladle liquid and vegetables into strainer, and return liquid to saucepan. Set aside. Remove Chinese mushrooms from strainer, and discard remaining vegetables. Use a sharp paring knife to remove stems from mushrooms and discard. Cut mushrooms into paper-thin slices. Add to liquid.

Bring soup to a simmer over medium-high heat. Place softened butter and flour in a small mixing bowl, and mix thoroughly with a fork, making sure all flour is absorbed. Ladle ½ cup soup into bowl and stir mixture until smooth. Pour into pan, stir, and simmer about 2 minutes. Add cream and port, stir, and heat through. Add salt and pepper to taste. Ladle into individual bowls and garnish with minced parsley.

 *Dried Chinese or Japanese black mushrooms are usually available in a well-stocked supermarket. Fresh shiitake mushrooms can be substituted. Remove stems, wipe or brush mushrooms clean, thinly slice, and add to soup after straining broth.*

※

Hoisin-Grilled Pork Tenderloin

SERVES 8

THIS IS ONE of the easiest to prepare, and classiest cuts of meat that you can serve your honored guests. Pork tenderloin is like beef tenderloin–exceedingly tender and full of flavor. Sold two per bag in most markets, pork tenderloins are about 1 pound each and can be dressed up with a fancy sauce or served straight off the grill proudly unsauced, as we do here.

> 2 pork tenderloins (about 2 pounds total)
> ⅓ cup hoisin sauce (see Cook's Notes)
> 1 tablespoon dry sherry
> Freshly ground black pepper, to taste

Tenderloins are partially covered by a very thin membrane of gristle, called silverskin, which needs to be removed. Dry tenderloins with a paper towel. Use a sharp boning knife or pointed 4-inch paring knife to remove silverskin. Hold knife horizontally with edge of blade facing small end of meat and slip it under silverskin. Keep blade angled just slightly toward gristle, rather than meat, and cut through toward "tail" of tenderloin, which will lift a flap of gristle. Hold on to flap, reverse position of knife, and use it to peel away gristle toward large end of tenderloin. Repeat to peel all gristle from meat surface, always keeping knife angled slightly toward silverskin to avoid wasting meat.

In a small mixing bowl, combine hoisin sauce, sherry, and a few grinds black pepper. Coat tenderloins with sauce. Set aside on a plate or platter. Prepare a charcoal fire or preheat a gas grill (page 108). When the fire is medium-hot, place tenderloins on grill rack. Cover grill, and cook, turning once, until an instant-read thermometer registers 150°F when inserted in thickest part of meat, about 12 minutes. Hold tenderloins in a warm, not hot, oven while you grill asparagus. Cut tenderloins diagonally in slices about ¼ inch, arrange on plates, and serve at once.

Cook's Notes

 *Hoisin sauce is a bottled Chinese-style barbecue sauce found in the Asian section of supermarkets.*

※

Grilled Asparagus

SERVES 8

ASPARAGUS is seldom better than when simply grilled. Pencil-thin varieties don't need to be peeled. Some people don't peel the thick stalks, although we think they cook more uniformly when peeled.

> About 2 pounds asparagus, cut uniformly into
>   5- to 6-inch lengths (see Cook's Notes)
> 2 tablespoons olive oil
> Salt and freshly ground black pepper, to taste

In a 9-by-13-inch baking dish or a large mixing bowl, roll

asparagus in olive oil with your hands to coat stalks thoroughly. Use tongs or a long, flat metal spatula to spread asparagus on grill rack over a medium-hot fire. Sprinkle with salt and a few grinds pepper. Cook 2 to 3 minutes, turn, season, and cook until crisp-tender, 2 to 3 minutes longer. Place on plates alongside pork tenderloin.

COOK'S NOTES

➤ *Buy asparagus with tight, fresh-looking tips. Tips that are opening like flowers or are soft and mushy indicate stalks past their prime. Rinse tips well under running water to dislodge any sandy soil.*

❋

Caramel Ice Cream Pie

SERVES 10

THIS IS A NATURAL do-ahead dessert. Use top-quality ice cream. Vanilla and coffee are our favorites.

Crust
Nonstick cooking spray, for coating
1 cup Post brand Grape-Nuts cereal
¼ cup pecan pieces
¼ cup granulated sugar
¼ teaspoon ground cinnamon
Pinch salt
3 tablespoons unsalted butter, melted

Caramel Sauce
1 cup granulated sugar
¼ cup plus 2 tablespoons water
½ cup whipping cream

2 pints vanilla ice cream

¼ cup pecans, toasted and coarsely chopped, for garnish

Preheat oven to 375°F. Spray a 9-inch pie pan with nonstick cooking spray.

To make crust, place Grape-Nuts in a food processor fitted with the metal blade. Process until fine crumbs are formed, 2 minutes. Add pecans, sugar, cinnamon, and salt. Process 30 seconds longer. Add melted butter and process until just incorporated. Transfer to prepared pie pan. Press crumbs firmly into bottom and sides of pan. Bake until lightly brown and crisp, 10 to 12 minutes. Cool completely on a wire rack.

To make caramel sauce, blend sugar and ¼ cup water in a deep, heavy, 1-quart saucepan. Bring to a boil over medium-high heat, stirring occasionally. Brush down sides of pan with a wet pastry brush to prevent sugar from crystallizing. Boil, without stirring, until sugar mixture turns deep amber, 10 to 12 minutes. Watch closely, as mixture can quickly go from amber to burnt. Remove from heat and carefully add whipping cream and 2 tablespoons water. Stand back to avoid spattering. Place over low heat and stir with a wooden spoon until all caramel is dissolved, 3 to 5 minutes. Let cool.

To assemble pie, remove 1 pint of ice cream from freezer to refrigerator 30 to 40 minutes before beginning assembly. At the same time, place cooled crust in freezer. Spread softened ice cream over chilled pie crust. Top with half of cooled caramel sauce. Return to freezer for 1 to 2 hours before repeating with second pint of ice cream. Top pie with toasted pecans, cover with oiled plastic wrap, and freeze until firm or for at least 4 hours. Transfer from freezer to refrigerator 15 to 20 minutes before serving to soften slightly.

Another Four-Course Dinner

SERVES 10

✳ ✳ ✳

PENNE WITH GARLIC AND TOASTED BREAD CRUMBS
(not pictured)

GREEN BEANS WITH WALNUT VINAIGRETTE

ROASTED CORNISH GAME HENS WITH FRESH HERBS

MUSHROOM RICE PILAF

FRESH APPLE CAKE

✳

Suggested wines:
CHARDONNAY WITH PASTA COURSE, MERLOT WITH ENTRÉE

✳

✳ *PLANNING AHEAD* ✳

- 1 to 2 weeks in advance, make and freeze apple cake.

- 1 day in advance, thaw game hens, if frozen, in refrigerator.

- The morning of serving, thaw cake at room temperature. Prepare and cook green beans and toast walnuts for salad. Prepare game hens for roasting.

- 2 hours in advance, make rice pilaf. Make salad dressing. Toast bread crumbs and chop garlic and anchovies for pasta sauce.

- About 1½ hours before serving entrée, preheat oven to 375°F.

- 1 hour in advance, roast game hens.

- 30 minutes in advance, boil water for pasta. Warm bowls or plates for pasta and plates for entrée. Remove green beans from refrigerator.

- Just before serving, cook pasta, reheat bread crumbs, and finish dish. Reheat rice. Toss salad just before serving.

THIS MENU, except for the dessert (which we recommend making ahead), is a breeze to put together in one day. This is easy Saturday-night entertaining at its best. Shop on Friday after work, then leisurely review the Planning Ahead steps on Saturday. We often suggest setting the table the day before a party, but for this menu, you'll have plenty of time to set it the day of the party.

This menu is terrific for cool-weather entertaining. The pasta course has the gutsy flavors of garlic and anchovies, and is followed by a crisp green bean and walnut salad. Walnut oil lends a sweet subtleness to the salad. We blend lots of fresh herbs, a hint of mustard, and the woodsy taste of cremini mushrooms for our rice and game hen entrée. A hint of lemon with the fresh taste of apples makes the cake a perfect finish to the meal.

Our intent, for this menu, is to have all courses plated and garnished in the kitchen. For the nuts and bolts of setup, you'll need plates or bowls for the pasta, small plates for the salad, large plates for the entrée, and dessert plates. Yep, that's a lot of plates. If you don't have enough, either wash the salad plates to use for dessert or borrow extras. For each guest, you'll need to set a napkin, a knife, a spoon, and three forks—one for the pasta and salad, another for the entrée, and a third for dessert. The forks used for the first and second courses can be washed before serving dessert. Table decorations can be as simple as soft glowing candles. Or with a little flair, you can arrange a still life of wintry fruits and evergreens. We won't wax too poetic here, but you get the idea.

Penne with Garlic and Toasted Bread Crumbs

SERVES 10

THE ITALIANS serve pasta mainly as a first course, which makes a great way to start a slightly formal meal. This pasta is delicious and not too filling. We encourage you to take a few minutes to crumble your own bread crumbs from a loaf of fresh bread, rather than use commercial crumbs. It is these crumbs, toasted in olive oil, that give this dish its special taste and texture.

¾ cup extra-virgin olive oil
2½ cups loosely packed fresh bread crumbs
3 large cloves garlic, peeled and minced
9 anchovy filets, minced
2 tablespoons salt
1½ pounds dried penne
Freshly ground black pepper, to taste

Fill an 8- to 10-quart stockpot two-thirds full of water, cover, and bring to boil over high heat. Divide olive oil between 2 frying pans, one 10-inch pan and one 8-inch pan. Place larger pan over medium heat, add bread crumbs, and cook, stirring frequently, until they are crisp and brown, 20 to 25 minutes.

Heat oil in smaller pan over medium heat. Add garlic and anchovy filets, and cook until garlic begins to sizzle. Allow garlic to brown slightly, but be careful not to burn it.

When pasta water has reached a boil, add salt and then pasta. Stir to prevent sticking and cook pasta until al dente (with a little bite remaining). Pasta shouldn't be mushy, but if it still has a crunchy, raw center, cook 1 to 2 minutes longer. Drain pasta thoroughly in a colander. Leave about ¼ cup pasta cooking water in bottom of stockpot to use as part of sauce.

Return pasta to pot with reserved cooking water. Add garlic-anchovy mixture and bread crumbs. Toss well and divide among individual plates or bowls. Top each portion with a couple grinds of black pepper. Serve immediately, while crumbs are crisp.

✳

Green Beans with Walnut Vinaigrette

SERVES 10

THIS RECIPE will require a trip to a specialty store for the walnut oil, if you cannot find it in a well-stocked supermarket. It will be well worth your efforts. Walnut oil has a delicate, buttery nut flavor that lingers sweetly on the palate. Because there are so few ingredients in this recipe, the quality of the green beans is critical. Taste a bean before you buy. It should be crisp and tender. If you can find the French green beans labeled "haricots verts," spend the extra money and buy them—they are fabulous. This salad is equally delicious if you substitute pencil-thin asparagus or sugar snap peas.

1¾ pounds young, tender green beans
1 tablespoon plus ⅛ teaspoon salt
1 cup chopped walnuts
1 tablespoon walnut oil (see Cook's Notes)

Vinaigrette
½ cup walnut oil
3 tablespoons rice wine vinegar (see Cook's Notes)
1 teaspoon granulated sugar
¾ teaspoon salt
1 tablespoon minced shallots
Freshly ground black pepper, to taste

Fill an 8- to 10-quart stockpot three-quarters full with water, cover, and bring to a boil over high heat. Rinse beans thoroughly and trim off stem ends. Prepare a large bowl of ice water (use lots of ice), and set aside.

When water comes to a boil, add 1 tablespoon salt. Add beans and blanch just until beans are crisp-tender, 2 to 4 minutes. Keep tasting for doneness; beans should be brilliant green and very crisp, but not raw. Immediately drain beans in a colander and plunge into ice water for no longer than 1 to 2 minutes. Drain, then wrap in several layers of paper towel, place in a plastic bag, and refrigerate until 30 minutes before serving.

To toast walnuts, preheat oven to 325°F. Place walnuts on a rimmed baking sheet. Pour walnut oil over nuts, add ⅛ teaspoon salt, and toss to combine. Spread nuts in a single layer and bake until barely golden, 10 to 15 minutes. Let cool. Set aside at room temperature until ready to serve.

To make vinaigrette, combine walnut oil, rice wine vinegar, sugar, salt, shallots, and pepper to taste. Set aside until ready to serve.

Just before serving, place beans in a medium mixing bowl and toss with dressing. Divide among individual salad plates, and garnish with toasted walnuts.

COOK'S NOTES

~ *Once opened, walnut oil must be stored in the refrigerator. It will keep for several months. Use walnut oil with other salads, such as curly endive, toasted walnuts, and pears or butter lettuce, julienned apple, and fennel. Toss pasta with walnut oil, toasted walnuts, and fresh herbs. Experiment—that's when cooking is fun.*

~ *Rice wine vinegar can be found in the Asian section of well-stocked supermarkets. It is available regular and seasoned—buy the regular style.*

※

Roasted Cornish Game Hens with Fresh Herbs

SERVES 10

SERVING LITTLE WHOLE BIRDS such as quail or poussin (very young chicken) is an elegant but simple way to approach entertaining. Specialty markets are usually required to find either of these expensive birds, but nearly every supermarket has affordable Cornish game hens, most often in the freezer case. They provide the elegance of a whole bird on each plate, while avoiding the cook's possible bankruptcy! Dijon-style mustard blended with fresh herbs, salt, and pepper gives the hens a brightly flavored coating.

10 Cornish game hens (about 18 ounces each),
    thawed (see Cook's Notes)
½ cup loosely packed fresh tarragon leaves
    (about 1 medium bunch), minced
1 cup loosely packed fresh flat-leaf parsley leaves
    (about 1 medium bunch), minced
1 cup Dijon-style mustard
1½ teaspoons salt
Freshly ground black pepper, to taste

Preheat oven to 375°F. Remove giblets from hens and reserve for another use. Rinse each bird inside and out under cold running water, and dry with paper towels. Line 1 or 2 baking pans (about 12 by 16 inches) on which the birds will fit with aluminum foil to make cleanup easier. Place a roasting rack or a baker's wire rack in pan. In a small mixing bowl, combine herbs, mustard, salt, and plenty of freshly ground pepper. Use your hands to spread mixture evenly over birds. Arrange birds breast side up on rack. Roast until thigh juices run clear when pricked with a small knife or an instant-read thermometer inserted between thigh and body registers 170°F, about 1 hour. Allow to rest 5 minutes before serving on individual plates with rice pilaf.

COOK'S NOTES

↘ *Thaw frozen birds for 2 days in refrigerator or under very slowly running cold water in a large pot for several hours.*

✻
Mushroom Rice Pilaf

SERVES 10

FOR THIS PILAF we use basmati rice, the nutty-flavored, long-grain rice grown in India and surrounding areas. Texas has also been a producer, with the rice labeled "Texmati." We love this rice not only for its flavor, but also for its firm texture. More and more, this rice is available in well-stocked supermarkets. If you can find the brown button mushrooms called cremini, buy them. They have a more pronounced earthy flavor than white button mushrooms and will enhance the pilaf. You can substitute white button mushrooms or, if you like, use morel, shiitake, or chanterelle mushrooms, or a combination.

2½ cups basmati rice

5 tablespoons vegetable oil

1 large yellow onion (about 10 ounces),
    peeled and finely chopped

2 cloves garlic, peeled and minced

1 pound fresh cremini mushrooms, wiped or
    brushed clean, stems trimmed, and sliced

1 tablespoon fresh thyme leaves or 2 teaspoons
    dried thyme

2 teaspoons salt

3½ cups Chicken Stock (page 46) or 1¾ cans
    (16 ounces each) low-sodium chicken broth

½ cup minced fresh parsley

Preheat oven to 325°F. Place rice in a medium mixing bowl, cover with cold water, and swish rice around with your hands. Drain water by tilting bowl and holding back rice with your hand. Repeat 2 more times. On the final washing, drain rice very well, and set aside.

Heat a straight-sided, 6-quart frying pan with oven-proof handles over medium-high heat. When hot, add oil. Tilt pan to spread oil, then add onion and garlic. Sauté, stirring frequently, until onion begins to soften, about 3 minutes. Add mushrooms and sauté for 3 to 4 minutes. Add thyme, salt, and rice, and sauté, stirring constantly, until rice is coated with oil and turns whitish, 2 to 3 minutes. Add stock or broth, raise heat to high, and cook, uncovered, until all stock or broth on surface of rice disappears and small holes form, about 5 minutes. Cover pan with a tight-fitting lid and place in preheated oven for 20 minutes. Taste rice; it should be tender, but still slightly firm. Bake longer if necessary.

When ready to serve, stir minced parsley into rice and transfer to a serving bowl.

COOK'S NOTES

➤ *The rice reheats well if made ahead. Warm in a preheated 300°F oven or covered in a microwave.*

Fresh Apple Cake

SERVES 12

THIS SIMPLE, yet simply delicious apple cake looks elegant at a sit-down dinner and feels comfortable at a backyard barbecue. Lemon, the only added flavor, gives just the right spark. It is best to peel, core, and dice the apples just before adding to the batter so they do not turn brown.

    2 sticks (8 ounces) unsalted butter, plus
        butter for coating pan
    2 cups granulated sugar
    3 large eggs
    2 teaspoons pure vanilla extract
    Grated zest of 1 medium to large lemon,
        plus 2 to 3 tablespoons juice
    3 cups all-purpose flour
    1 teaspoon baking powder
    ½ teaspoon baking soda
    Pinch salt
    ½ cup buttermilk
    2 large, tart, firm apples (about 1 pound),
        such as Granny Smith or Newton, peeled,
        cored, and cut into ½-inch dice
    1 cup powdered sugar

Preheat oven to 350°F. Butter a 10-inch springform pan. In a large mixing bowl, cream butter and sugar with an electric mixer until light and fluffy. Add eggs, 1 at a time, mixing well after each addition. Add vanilla and grated lemon zest, and mix well. Add 1½ cups of the flour, baking powder, baking soda, and salt. Mix until just incorporated. Add buttermilk, and stir well. Add the remaining 1½ cups flour and stir to blend. Add diced apples and stir until blended. Pour batter into prepared pan, and spread it to sides of pan with a rubber spatula. Batter will be thick.

Bake until cake is golden brown and a toothpick or cake tester inserted in middle of cake comes out clean, 50 to 55 minutes. Let cool.

In a small mixing bowl, stir together powdered sugar and 2 tablespoons lemon juice. Add more lemon juice as needed to produce a glaze that will run just enough to cover top of cake without pouring down sides. Top cooled cake with glaze, using a rubber spatula to spread it nearly to the edges.

When cool, remove sides from pan. Transfer cake to a serving platter. Cake holds well, tightly wrapped in plastic wrap, for up to 3 days at room temperature. It can be frozen, well wrapped, for up to 3 weeks. Thaw completely at room temperature before serving.

CHAPTER 4

Brunches

✳ ✳ ✳

Eggs, Bacon, and Potatoes

Jewish-Style Brunch

Easter Brunch

✳

ADVANTAGES to entertaining during the daytime include the fact that your guests are awake and so are you! The demands of our daily lives sometimes leave little energy for evening entertaining. A late-morning or early-afternoon weekend gathering prevents guests from worrying when the baby-sitter has to be home or what time they need to be up the next morning for a business meeting.

Brunches also offer the opportunity to put together fun and eclectic meals. There are few rules when planning a brunch menu. All dishes, both savory and sweet, are generally served at once. The style is relaxed and casual.

It is easy to build brunch menus around a theme. Our first theme is a hearty American one. Put the yogurt and granola aside for a day and have a real Eggs, Bacon, and Potatoes Brunch. Everyone one will smile at real sunnyside-up eggs, thick sliced bacon, and great potato pancakes. We interpret some great food traditions with our Jewish-Style Brunch. The blintzes, applesauce, and rugelach take a little advance work and planning, but are well worth it. The rest of the menu—arranging platters of silken lox, fresh tomatoes, and onions, and finding the best bagels a local bakery has to offer—comes together in a flash.

The Easter Brunch is a bit more elaborate. A wonderful egg and mushroom casserole is accompanied by excellent ham and an asparagus salad. To further celebrate the occasion we offer a luscious Caramel Pecan Bread Pudding that is served with the fresh strawberries of the season. We recommend serving the brunch buffet style, but would dress up this special-occasion menu by using fine china and linen and accenting the table with fresh flowers.

For any brunch, it is much easier for the host if all beverages are prepared in advance. Coffee can be in thermal containers, and juice, if serving, in pitchers so guests can help themselves.

Wake up and smell the coffee! Enjoy a relaxed morning with good friends and good food.

Eggs, Bacon, and Potatoes

SERVES 8

✳ ✳ ✳

POTATO PANCAKES WITH
APPLE SALSA

BAKED THICK-SLICED BACON

SUNNYSIDE-UP EGGS
(DONE RIGHT!)

✳

Suggested beverages:
FRESH FRUIT SPRITZERS (PAGE 17),
FRESHLY SQUEEZED ORANGE JUICE,
AND COFFEE

✳

✳ *PLANNING AHEAD* ✳

◉ 1 week in advance, make and freeze potato pan-cakes.

◉ The morning of the brunch, make apple salsa. Thaw potato pancakes.

◉ 1 hour in advance, preheat oven to 350°F.

◉ 45 minutes in advance, cook bacon. Lower oven temperature to 250°F for warming food.

◉ 20 minutes in advance, fry potato pancakes.

◉ Just before serving, reheat bacon, and make eggs.

WELL, LET'S CALL a spade a spade–this menu is cholesterol city. We know it, you know it, your personal trainer will know it (invite him or her to brunch!). Some-times you just have to indulge–so enjoy. Have a salad for dinner, have water for dinner, have a glass of red wine (the French Diet theory), but eat the real stuff. Nutri-tion is a matter of balance. None of us eats this type of food every day for breakfast, but on a special Sunday with friends, it's a great treat.

This menu is our interpretation of breakfast clas-sics. Potato pancakes are crisp and thin, served with our zesty apple salsa. Baking bacon in the oven is easy, less messy, and convenient for the cook. This leaves the last-minute focus where it should be–cooking perfect eggs. Your guests will love the refreshing fruit spritzers.

We designed this menu so you wouldn't have to get up at 6 A.M. to prepare it. We certainly suggest you do the grocery shopping ahead, but there will be plenty of time to set the table the day of the brunch. Nothing fancy here, just a knife, a fork, and a spoon for each guest.

Have coffee mugs and glasses for juice on the table, but serve the entrée from the kitchen. You'll want to have entrée plates warmed in advance. Colorful napkins and a pitcher of flowers would be great. Keep the coffee com-ing, and your guests will be happy to settle in for some good conversation and fun.

Potato Pancakes with Apple Salsa

SERVES 8

NO GUEST has ever turned us down when presented with these crisp, thin pancakes fried in a very hot skillet. The apple salsa accompanying these pancakes makes for a wonderful flavor complement. Think of using this salsa paired with other foods, such as grilled fish or pork tenderloin, or leftover grilled chicken to make tacos.

Apple Salsa

2 tablespoons olive oil or vegetable oil

½ teaspoon ground coriander

½ teaspoon ground cumin

3 large, crisp apples, such as Braeburn, Gala, Fuji, or Granny Smith (see Cook's Notes)

2 tablespoons freshly squeezed lime juice

½ cup diced red onion

½ cup chopped fresh cilantro leaves

1 fresh jalapeño chili, seeded, deveined, and minced (see Cook's Notes)

Pinch salt

Potato Pancakes

2 pounds russet potatoes, peeled and rinsed under cold water

1 medium yellow onion (about 5 ounces), peeled

1 large egg, beaten

1 teaspoon salt

Freshly ground black pepper, to taste

Vegetable oil, for frying

To make salsa, in a small frying pan over medium-high heat, heat oil, coriander, and cumin until hot. (You will begin to smell the spices.) Set aside.

Halve and core apples, but do not peel. Chop apples into ¼-inch dice, and place in a medium mixing bowl. Add lime juice, which will keep apples from browning. Add red onion, cilantro, jalapeño, salt, and spiced oil. Mix to combine. Cover salsa and set aside until serving; it is best made 1 to 2 hours ahead.

To make pancakes, coarsely grate potatoes and onion using a box grater or a food processor fitted with the grating disk. Place vegetables in a colander and use your hands or back of a spoon to squeeze out as much liquid as possible. Transfer to a large mixing bowl. Add egg, salt, and a few grinds of pepper, and mix to combine.

Pour enough oil into 1 or 2 heavy, 10- or 12-inch frying pans (preferably cast iron) to cover bottom of pan by ⅛ inch. Heat oil over medium-high heat until hot but not smoking. Scoop about ¼ cup potato mixture and place in pan. Use a spatula to flatten mixture to form a pancake. Form as many pancakes in the pan as will comfortably fit without crowding. Fry on one side until golden brown. Turn with a spatula, and brown other side. Adjust heat as needed. Remove to paper towels to drain. Continue making pancakes, adding more oil as needed. Serve immediately, or keep warm in a 250°F oven.

COOK'S NOTES

⌁ *Of all the apples suggested, we prefer to use Braeburn. These red-skinned apples make the salsa pretty and offer a nice color contrast for the plate. They are also quite crisp.*

One fresh jalapeño chili makes this salsa quite lively. If you don't like the heat, try ½ jalapeño, or omit entirely. Be sure to wash your hands immediately after handling chilies, so you will not inadvertently touch and irritate your eyes.

We prefer the texture of potatoes grated on a box grater, but they taste great either way.

The cooked pancakes can also be frozen for up to 1 month. Layer the pancakes between sheets of waxed paper in a covered freezer container. To reheat, place frozen pancakes on baking sheets and crisp in a pre-heated 400° F oven for about 20 minutes.

✳

Baked Thick-Sliced Bacon

SERVES 8

IN THE UNITED STATES there is no meat more associated with breakfast or brunch than bacon—slices of cured, smoked pork belly—and no more common method of cooking bacon these days than microwaving. But if a lot of bacon needs to be cooked, the easiest way to get the job done is roasting it in a baking pan in the oven. You may do it hours or even three or four days in advance, and refrigerate, covered with plastic wrap. Reheat at the last minute, just as most restaurants do.

Prepackaged bacon found in the deli cases in supermarkets commonly has about eighteen to twenty-two slices per pound. If you buy bacon labeled "thick sliced" or have the butcher slice regular or "pepper" bacon (cured with cracked black pepper as well as the usual sugar and salt), you'll get fewer slices per pound, but have something more substantial to chew on. So figure out how many slices to buy by deciding how many slices per person you wish to offer for brunch. Three slices per guest will likely be close.

24 thick slices bacon (1½ to 2 pounds total)

Preheat oven to 350° F. Line a 10-by-15-inch baking pan with aluminum foil to make cleanup easier or use a non-stick pan. The pan should have at least ½-inch sides to contain melting fat. Arrange bacon in tight, nonoverlapping rows in pan. Bake until crisp to your liking, 20 minutes or longer. Use tongs or a metal spatula to transfer to a plate lined with paper towels. Repeat, if necessary, to cook all the bacon. Bacon may be reheated in a preheated 200° F oven for 10 minutes, or in a microwave on high power for about 30 seconds before serving.

COOK'S NOTES

Baking bacon renders fabulously full-flavored cooking fat, which you can save. Pour the hot fat from the pan through a fine strainer into a heatproof storage container. Store in refrigerator for up to 3 months, and use to sauté potatoes or onions.

✳︎
Sunnyside-Up Eggs (Done Right!)

SERVES 8

PEOPLE WHO LOVE the taste of eggs—meaning egg yolks, really—usually like their eggs done one of several ways: scrambled softly, poached, soft-boiled, "over easy," or "up," often called "sunnyside up." The common theme in these preparations is that the egg white is cooked until it is set, but the yolk remains soft and liquid. Egg lovers so crave the taste of the warm but not solid yolks that some of them hoard the yolk until the last minute. One thing you can count on is that your guests will respect you for offering them up-style eggs, which are easier to prepare than most cooks think. A decent 12-inch nonstick frying pan, with lid, and a thin-bladed metal or plastic spatula are the tools needed. A well-seasoned cast-iron frying pan is a classic tool too, of course.

2 tablespoons unsalted butter or vegetable oil
16 large eggs, room temperature
Salt and freshly ground black pepper, to taste
Freshly chopped parsley, for garnish
1 small bottle ketchup (optional)
1 small bottle hot-pepper sauce (optional)

Gently warm a large serving platter on which to serve eggs. Heat frying pan over medium heat for 1 to 2 minutes, add butter or oil, then reduce heat to medium-low. When butter has melted, crack eggs into pan, 4 or 5 at a time, without crowding. Season with salt and pepper. Sprinkle 1 tablespoon water around edge of pan and cover—the water turns to steam, which helps cook top of eggs, eliminating the need to turn them. Cook, covered, 1 to 2 minutes, then check eggs—they are done when whites are set on top and yolks are still runny. Remove eggs to serving platter and continue cooking remaining portions. Sprinkle a little parsley over eggs just before serving. Accompany with ketchup and hot-pepper sauce, if desired.

Jewish-Style
Brunch

SERVES 8

❋ ❋ ❋

LOX AND BAGELS, TOMATOES,
RED ONION, AND CREAM CHEESE

BLINTZES AND SOUR CREAM

HOMEMADE APPLESAUCE

RUGELACH
(not pictured)

❋

Suggested beverages:
TOMATO JUICE,
FRESHLY SQUEEZED
ORANGE OR GRAPEFRUIT JUICE,
COFFEE

❋

- ◉ 1 week in advance, make and refrigerate apple-sauce. Make and freeze unbaked rugelach.

- ◉ 2 days in advance, make, assemble (but do not cook), and refrigerate blintzes.

- ◉ The morning of the brunch, buy bagels. Bake rugelach. Arrange lox on a platter with tomatoes and red onions; refrigerate until serving.

- ◉ 20 minutes in advance, sauté or bake blintzes. Set out applesauce, sour cream, cream cheese, and lox.

- ◉ Just before serving slice and toast bagels.

SOME OF US GREW UP eating these wonderful foods, while others have never known this combination of tastes (let alone being able to pronounce rugelach–it's *ROO-ge-lah*). Memories of this type of brunch always involved lots of lively conversations, platters and plates being busily passed, then a lull and quiet as we began eating. Of course, everyone wanted seconds.

There are a couple of ways you can serve this meal. Set the table simply–a napkin, a knife, a fork, and a spoon for each guest will do. Have a large platter for the lox, tomatoes, and red onion. You'll need a small bowl for the cream cheese and a basket for the bagels. The blintzes and rugelach will require platters, and bowls will be needed for the sour cream, jam, and applesauce. Either pass platters and eat family style, or have all the food on a buffet, with plates in a stack, and let your guests pick and choose. Remember to warm the plates and the platter for the blintzes. Have pitchers of juice on the table, or serve it ahead. Coffee served with the meal would be great.

Lox and Bagels, Tomatoes, Red Onion, and Cream Cheese

SERVES 8

THERE IS A RITUAL to eating lox and bagels. The ingredients are prepared and laid out on platters. One cuts a bagel in half, spreads cream cheese on the bagel halves, lays slices of lox on top, followed by a few rings of red onion, then a slice of tomato. It is easier to eat this open face, but that is a personal preference. A few capers are nice, but a little frou-frou. And please, no sprouts.

> 1 to 1½ pounds lox (see Cook's Notes)
> 2 or 3 ripe tomatoes (about 12 ounces), cored
>   and thinly sliced
> 1 large red onion (about 10 ounces), peeled
>   and thinly sliced
> 12 fresh bagels (see Cook's Notes)
> 8 ounces cream cheese

Arrange lox, slices overlapping, on a large serving platter with tomato and onion slices. Cut bagels in half (or let guests cut their own) and serve in a bread basket. Place cream cheese in a ramekin or small bowl.

COOK'S NOTES

〜 *There is no getting around the fact that good lox is expensive. Serving it is a generous treat, and your guests will know it. For each serving, we suggest 2 or 3 slices.*

〜 *Lots of bagel flavors would work well: plain, sesame, poppy seed, onion, garlic, whole wheat, and rye. This is not the place for cinnamon-raisin, blueberry, and other sweet flavors!*

❋
Blintzes and Sour Cream

MAKES 24 BLINTZES; SERVES 8

CHEESE BLINTZES are simply thin pancakes (crepes), filled with a slightly sweet cottage cheese mixture, folded, then either lightly browned in a skillet or baked in an oven. This is real comfort food–children adore them, and adults love them. A dollop of sour cream and/or a dollop of berry jam makes blintzes divine.

Crepe

1½ cups all-purpose flour, sifted

1 teaspoon salt

2 teaspoons baking powder

4 large eggs

1⅓ cups milk

Filling

16 ounces dry-curd cottage cheese or farmer's cheese (see Cook's Notes)

16 ounces small-curd cottage cheese

3 large egg yolks

⅓ cup granulated sugar

Pinch salt

1 teaspoon pure vanilla extract

2 tablespoons vegetable oil, or more as needed

1 tablespoon unsalted butter, or more as needed

2 cups sour cream

1 cup seedless berry jam, such as raspberry or strawberry

To make crepe batter, sift flour with salt and baking powder into a large mixing bowl. In a medium mixing bowl, beat eggs, then add milk and 1 cup of water. Use a mixing spoon or whisk to make a well in dry ingredients, pour in liquid ingredients, and combine with a few swift strokes. Ignore lumps; they will dissolve when batter is stirred. Let batter rest for 30 minutes at room temperature.

To make filling, in a food processor fitted with the metal blade or in a blender, combine cheeses, egg yolks, sugar, salt, and vanilla. Process to purée, about 1 minute. Remove to a medium bowl, cover, and refrigerate.

To make crepes, heat an 8-inch, nonstick (highly recommended) frying pan (see Cook's Notes) over medium-high heat. Place a drop of water in pan. If it sizzles, pan is ready. Fold a paper towel into quarters, spoon 1 tablespoon of the vegetable oil onto towel, and use to lightly oil pan each time you make a crepe. Allow about 3 tablespoons batter per crepe (use a ¼ cup measuring cup filled three-quarters full). Pour batter into pan. Working quickly, tilt pan so batter evenly coats bottom and part way up sides. Cook each crepe on one side until lightly browned. Loosen with a spatula, turn, and cook just a few seconds on other side. Remove to a wire rack to cool. Continue making crepes. As crepes cool, stack between sheets of waxed paper.

To assemble blintzes, place ¼ cup filling in center of each crepe. Fold envelope style to form a rectangle. First fold bottom of crepe over filling. Fold over 2 sides, then top. Turn blintz so seam is on bottom.

To cook blintzes, preheat oven to 200°F. Heat a 12-inch frying pan over medium heat. Add the remaining 1 tablespoon oil and butter. Tilt pan to coat bottom, then add as many blintzes as will comfortably fit without crowding pan. Sauté until nicely browned on one side.

Turn blintzes with a spatula, and brown on other side. Use additional oil and butter as needed for cooking remaining blintzes. Place blintzes on a baking sheet in oven to keep warm. To serve, place blintzes on a platter, and accompany with sour cream and jam in small bowls.

COOK'S NOTES

~ *Dry-curd cottage cheese, also called farmer's cheese, can usually be found along with cottage cheese in the dairy case of a supermarket. If you can't find it, a reasonable substitute would be to use 32 ounces ricotta instead of the two types of cottage cheese.*

~ *Making crepes takes patience and some skill. If you ruin your first crepe throw it out and try again. A good-quality, nonstick frying pan will be your savior here. If you have only a 10-inch frying pan, spread crepe batter only on bottom of pan, not on sides.*

~ *You can bake blintzes instead of sautéing them. Place 1 inch apart on baking sheets and bake in a pre-heated 425°F oven until browned, about 20 minutes.*

~ *The blintzes can be assembled, but not sautéed or baked, and refrigerated for up to 2 days or frozen for up to 1 month. Place blintzes in a freezer container, layered between sheets of plastic wrap or waxed paper. Frozen blintzes should be thawed in the refrigerator before sautéing or baking. This keeps the filling from breaking the sides of the crepe.*

※

Homemade Applesauce

SERVES 10 TO 12

APPLESAUCE is so much better made from scratch and so very easy to do. We are deliberately not giving a measurement for sugar. Apples vary greatly in their sugar content, so taste to judge the sweetness level.

4 pounds apples, peeled, cored, and sliced
    in eighths (see Cook's Notes)
½ cup water
Sugar, to taste
2 teaspoons ground cinnamon

Place apple slices and the water in a heavy 4-quart saucepan over medium heat. Cover and cook, stirring frequently, until apples are soft and can be broken easily with a spoon, 25 to 30 minutes. You may need to reduce heat a bit if apples bubble too vigorously. (You don't want them to scorch on pan bottom.) We like to leave some soft chunks in our applesauce, but you can stir to achieve a completely smooth texture. Remove from heat.

Add sugar and cinnamon. We recommend starting with ⅓ cup sugar and then adding more as desired. Cool applesauce completely, then refrigerate. Applesauce can be refrigerated for up to 1 week. We don't recommend much longer than this; nor do we recommend freezing.

COOK'S NOTES

~ *Many different varieties of apples are available. Each will make a different style of applesauce. We particularly like Rome Beauties.*

Rugelach

MAKES 4 DOZEN RUGELACH

THE WORD *rugel* comes from the Yiddish, meaning "royal." Our ancestors brought recipes for these buttery little crescents when they came to this country. American cooks added cream cheese to the dough. We love the addition of semisweet chocolate to the filling, but you may omit it and increase the quantity of jam and walnuts by 2 tablespoons each.

2 sticks (8 ounces) unsalted butter, softened, plus more for coating baking sheets
8 ounces cream cheese, softened
¼ cup granulated sugar
1 teaspoon pure vanilla extract
2 cups all-purpose flour, plus more for dusting
¼ teaspoon salt
½ cup minced walnuts
½ cup apricot jam
6 ounces semisweet chocolate, minced or grated
1 egg, lightly beaten

In a large mixing bowl, beat butter and cream cheese together with an electric mixer. Add sugar and vanilla, and beat until fluffy. Add flour and salt, and mix completely. Dough will be sticky. Wrap dough in plastic wrap and refrigerate for at least 2 hours, or overnight.

Preheat oven to 350°F. Butter 2 baking sheets or use nonstick baking sheets. Divide dough into 4 equal pieces. If you have enough room to roll out 2 pieces of dough side by side, the work goes faster. Keep other 2 pieces refrigerated. Place walnuts, jam, and chocolate in separate small bowls by your work surface, along with small spoons for portioning each. Even after long chilling, dough can remain a bit sticky, so be sure to have plenty of flour on your hands while rolling out dough.

On a lightly floured work surface, roll each piece of dough into a circle 9- to 10-inches in diameter. Spread one-fourth of jam onto each circle with back of spoon. Do not worry if jam does not completely cover circle. Sprinkle each circle of dough with one-fourth of walnuts and one-fourth of chocolate. Concentrate more of these items toward outside of dough circle rather than center. They will move toward center as you roll dough.

With a sharp knife, cut each circle into 12 wedges. You may need to rinse knife blade with hot water once or twice to avoid sticking. Starting at wide end, roll each wedge, jelly-roll fashion. Bend roll slightly to make a crescent and place on baking sheets. Some filling will spill out as you roll. Scrape it up and sprinkle on wedges yet to be rolled. When finished with the first 2 circles, clean work surface of sticky dough and jam residue, and repeat process with remaining 2 pieces of dough.

Brush each rugelach with beaten egg and bake until deep golden brown, about 30 minutes. Remove to wire racks to cool completely.

COOK'S NOTES

➤ *A firm-bladed metal pastry scraper will help you loosen each wedge of dough from your counter or work surface as you begin to roll it with the filling. The scraper is also great for removing flour and sticky jam.*

➤ *Freeze Rugelach, unbaked, up to 1 month. Layer pastries between wax paper in lock-top plastic bags. Do not thaw before baking. Once baked, they keep well for 5 days, well wrapped.*

Easter Brunch

SERVES 8

✳ ✳ ✳

THICK-SLICED BLACK FOREST HAM
WITH APRICOT-MUSTARD CHUTNEY

BAKED EGG CASSEROLE WITH
ENGLISH MUFFINS

CHILLED ASPARAGUS SALAD

CARAMEL-PECAN BREAD PUDDING
(not pictured)

FRESH SEASONAL FRUIT

✳

Suggested beverages:
FRESHLY SQUEEZED ORANGE JUICE,
MIMOSAS (HALF ORANGE JUICE,
HALF CHAMPAGNE),
SPARKLING APPLE CIDER,
COFFEE, TEA

✳

- ◉ 1 to 2 weeks in advance, make and refrigerate chutney. Make and freeze bread pudding.

- ◉ 1 day in advance, prepare, assemble (but do not bake), and refrigerate casserole. Cook and refrigerate asparagus. Thaw bread pudding in refrigerator.

- ◉ The day of the brunch, make salad dressing. Arrange fruits on serving platter.

- ◉ 1 hour in advance, preheat oven to 375°F. Spoon chutney into serving bowl. Place asparagus on serving platter.

- ◉ 45 minutes in advance, bake egg casserole. Arrange ham slices in a baking pan. Portion bread pudding into individual baking dishes.

- ◉ 20 minutes in advance, lower oven temperature to 250°F. Heat ham and bread pudding.

- ◉ Just before serving, toast English muffins. Arrange ham slices on warmed serving platter. Dress salad.

THIS IS A GREAT do-ahead Easter brunch. There are too many other activities on Easter day to allow lots of time for cooking. Although this menu can be served family style, on a buffet, or at individual place settings, our vote is for buffet service. Here's why: The hot egg casserole requires a heatproof casserole holder with handles to pass it easily. At a buffet, the casserole stays put as guests help themselves. Also, if children are involved, they tend to be picky eaters, so a buffet gives them choices. Finally, all of these dishes, with their color and texture contrasts, look attractive on a buffet.

Our menu offers variety and great tastes. Ham is a classic for Easter, but offering the Black Forest-style ham served with this terrific chutney will be a surprising treat. Savory baked eggs with a hint of Dijon-style mustard and mushrooms are perfect served with toasted English muffins. We balance these dishes with asparagus and seasonal fruits. No one will pass up the bread pudding–who can resist.

For each serving style you'll need to set the table with a napkin, a knife, a fork, and a spoon for each guest. For a buffet, stack the plates on the serving table. For family style service, set the plates on the table. For serving individual plates, have the entrée plates warming in the kitchen. Set the salad out, arrange the plates, and serve. Make dessert a separate course served with coffee. Along with a lot to think about, there is a lot to enjoy.

❋

Thick-Sliced Black Forest Ham with Apricot Mustard Chutney

SERVES 8

YUM, WE LOVE this style of ham. Black Forest ham is a firm-textured, heavily smoked, slightly sweet ham with a dark exterior. Supermarkets sometimes stock it, or try a good-quality deli. If you have never tasted it, now is the time, especially with our Apricot Mustard Chutney. We developed the chutney using dried apricots so it can be made at any time of year. Making chutneys, jams, or relishes seems intimidating to beginning cooks, but it's just a matter of chopping, measuring, and combining ingredients, then cooking them on the stove top.

Chutney

1 pound dried apricots, cut into quarters

1 medium yellow onion (about 6 ounces), peeled
and cut into ¼-inch dice

1 large clove garlic, minced

¼ cup diced crystallized ginger (see Cook's Notes)

¼ cup dried currants or raisins

¾ cup packed light brown sugar

1 cup cider vinegar

¼ teaspoon crushed red pepper flakes

½ teaspoon salt

1 cinnamon stick (2 inches long)

2 teaspoons mustard seeds

8 to 10 (¼-inch thick) slices Black Forest
ham (about 2 pounds)

To make chutney, place apricots in a medium heatproof
bowl. Cover with 2 cups boiling water and let stand 15
minutes. In a 6-quart saucepan, combine all ingredients, including apricots and their soaking liquid. Bring
to a boil over medium-high heat. Reduce heat to maintain a simmer. Cook, uncovered, stirring occasionally,
until thickened, about 30 minutes. Let cool in pan. Discard cinnamon stick, transfer chutney to a glass jar, and
refrigerate. As with most chutneys, this one keeps well
for up to 6 months in the refrigerator.

To make ham, preheat oven to 250° F. Arrange ham
in a 9-by-13-inch baking pan. Cover with aluminum foil
and bake until heated through, 15 to 20 minutes.

COOK'S NOTES

🥢 *Crystallized ginger is typically found in the Asian
section of supermarkets. Look for it in a small 3- to 4-
ounce box. One box is sufficient for this recipe.*

❋

Baked Egg Casserole with English Muffins

SERVES 8

THIS CREAMY, tarragon-flavored casserole is a perfect match with the thick-sliced Black Forest ham, as
well as the asparagus salad.

10 tablespoons unsalted butter

2 cups coarse fresh bread crumbs

Nonstick cooking spray

1¼ pounds fresh mushrooms, wiped or brushed
clean, stems trimmed, and sliced ¼ inch thick

8 large hard-cooked eggs, sliced (see Cook's Notes)

1 medium onion (about 5 ounces), peeled and diced

½ cup all-purpose flour

4 cups whole milk

3 tablespoons Dijon-style mustard

1¼ teaspoons salt

Freshly ground black pepper, to taste

½ teaspoon freshly ground or grated nutmeg

1 bunch tarragon, leaves stripped off stems
and chopped

4 English muffins, split and toasted

Preheat oven to 325° F. Melt 2 tablespoons of the butter.
In a medium mixing bowl, toss fresh bread crumbs with
butter. Spread on a baking sheet and bake until crumbs
are lightly browned, about 10 minutes. Set aside. Raise
oven temperature to 375° F. Spray a 9-by-13-inch baking
dish with nonstick cooking spray.

Heat 2 tablespoons of the butter in a heavy, 12-inch
frying pan over medium-high heat until foam subsides.

Add mushrooms and cook, stirring frequently, until they have given up their moisture, and moisture has evaporated, about 10 minutes. Mushrooms should be dry. Spread mushrooms evenly over bottom of prepared baking dish. Spread sliced eggs on top of mushrooms.

In a heavy 3- or 4-quart saucepan over medium heat, melt the remaining 6 tablespoons butter. Add onion and sauté until soft but not browned, about 5 minutes. Reduce heat to medium-low, add flour, and stir carefully to break up as many lumps as possible. Cook, stirring regularly, until mixture is faintly colored, about 5 minutes. Raise heat to medium, add milk, and stir constantly to break up lumps while sauce thickens. Bring to a boil, reduce heat to a bare simmer, and cook for 5 minutes. Stir in mustard, salt, a few grinds pepper, nutmeg, and tarragon. Taste for seasoning and adjust if desired. Pour sauce evenly over top of mushroom-egg mixture and top with toasted bread crumbs.

Bake until casserole is bubbly, about 25 minutes. To serve, place a toasted English muffin half on each plate and spoon casserole on top.

COOK'S NOTES

To hard-cook eggs, pierce large end of each egg with sharp pin, point of thin, sharp knife, or point of skewer. This helps to prevent egg from cracking in water. Place eggs in saucepan, add cold water to cover, bring to a boil, reduce heat to a simmer, and cook 12 minutes. Drain, and bounce eggs a few times in pan to break shells. Cover with cold water, let stand for a few minutes, and peel.

✳
Chilled Asparagus Salad
SERVES 8

FROM OUR POINT OF VIEW, Easter brunch would not be complete without asparagus. It signals spring. A platter of bright green asparagus, tossed lightly with an orange vinaigrette, is the perfect accompaniment to this meal.

2 pounds asparagus
2 teaspoons salt

Vinaigrette
¼ teaspoon salt
⅛ teaspoon granulated sugar
Freshly ground black pepper, to taste
1 medium orange
2 tablespoons extra-virgin olive oil

Select a pan large enough to accommodate asparagus when lying flat. Fill pan about two-thirds full with water. Cover and bring to a boil over high heat. Grasp each asparagus spear about two-thirds down from tip. Snap or break off end, typically 1½ to 2 inches, and discard. Trim end of spear with a knife. Peel asparagus (not worth doing for pencil-thin asparagus) with a vegetable peeler: start at base of tip and peel toward bottom of spear to remove just the thin fibrous outer layer.

When water boils, add salt, then add asparagus. Cook, uncovered, for 3 minutes. Fill a large mixing bowl two-thirds full with ice water. Remove a spear and taste for doneness. The asparagus should be bright green and crisp-tender without tasting raw. If asparagus tastes raw, cook another minute or so, then taste again. When done, use tongs to remove asparagus and place immediately in ice water. Cool for 1 to 2 minutes, then place on a large plate or baking sheet lined with several layers of paper towels. If not using immediately, wrap in dry paper towels, enclose in a plastic bag, and refrigerate.

To make vinaigrette, combine salt, sugar, and a few grinds of pepper. Rinse and dry orange. Use a zester or vegetable peeler to remove zest from orange. Add 1 teaspoon to vinaigrette, and set aside 1 teaspoon for garnish. Extract juice from orange, measure 3 tablespoons, and add with olive oil. Mix, adjust to taste. Set aside.

To serve, place asparagus in a large mixing bowl, stir dressing, pour over asparagus, and lightly toss. Arrange on a serving platter, with spears aligned in one direction, and garnish with reserved orange zest.

COOK'S NOTES

➤ *Asparagus can be prepared a day ahead. We prefer to make the dressing the day of the party, so the orange juice in the dressing tastes fresh.*

✳

Caramel-Pecan Bread Pudding

SERVES 8

BREAD PUDDING is marvelous for a brunch. This is a great way to use stale bread. We top this pudding with melted Kraft caramels for an extra-special treat. If you prefer a heavier caramel topping, increase amount of caramels to 8 ounces.

1 cup chopped pecans, toasted
5 cups French bread cubes, ½-inch square
½ cup dark raisins
2 cups milk
1 cup whipping cream
5 large eggs
1 cup granulated sugar
1 tablespoon pure vanilla extract
6 ounces caramels
Maple syrup or corn syrup, as needed

Place toasted pecans, bread cubes, and raisins in an 8-inch-square baking dish. Toss to mix. In a medium mixing bowl, blend milk, cream, eggs, sugar, and vanilla. Use a whisk to blend eggs well. Pour egg mixture over bread cubes and allow to sit 15 minutes. Place in oven and bake until puffed and brown, 40 to 45 minutes.

In the meantime, melt caramels in a small, heavy saucepan over very low heat. If too thick to pour, thin them with a little maple or corn syrup. Pour melted caramels over hot pudding in a zigzag pattern. Allow pudding to cool completely, then refrigerate.

To rewarm, cut pudding into 8 servings. Place each serving in an individual ovenproof dish and warm in a preheated 350°F oven for 15 minutes.

COOK'S NOTES

➤ *The pudding can be well wrapped and frozen for up to 1 month. Thaw in refrigerator for 24 hours before rewarming. Rewarm as indicated above.*

CHAPTER 5

Outdoor Entertaining

✳ ✳ ✳

Barbecue—Ribs and Chicken, Coleslaw, and Corn

Seafood and Vegetables on the Grill

✳

*T*HE URGE TO BUILD A FIRE has been with mankind since the days prehistoric people first discovered that a piece of meat, singed over an open flame, had taste advantages compared with the same item raw, enabling prehistoric gourmets to extend their taste boundaries. Grilling couldn't be more popular today, as the curling trails of smoke all over America on any summer weekend attest. As an entertaining style, barbecuing or grilling is made for modern living. It is relaxed, fun, and unpretentious.

Our two outdoor menus are designed to keep you outdoors spending time with your guests. The barbecue is a real stick-to-your-ribs meal. Succulent baby back ribs are flavored with a dry rub. They share the spotlight with perfectly grilled chicken. The two accompanying salads can be made early in the day, along with the tasty cobbler.

In our second menu, we introduce you to the ease and delight of grilling fish and seafood. Just made for a healthy diet, the scallop kebobs are colorful and cook in a flash. The swordfish with hot-pepper sauce adds a wonderful zing. Couscous, grilled vegetables, and a luscious banana trifle complete the menu. Pull out the checkered tablecloth and keep the dinnerware casual. This might be the time for paper plates, as long as they are sturdy. This food is too good to be in your lap.

So, build your fire and enjoy a warm summer evening with friends.

About Grilling

❋   ❋   ❋

THERE ARE LITERALLY DOZENS of brands and styles of outdoor grills on the market. Our recipes assume that unless you have a gas grill, you own a charcoal-burning kettle-style grill with a vented lid. The racks are usually not adjustable for height, so the heat level is determined by how much charcoal is being used and how long it has burned, and by controlling the position of lid vents. Charcoal can be added through the openings provided next to rack handles on some grills; on others, you may need to lift the rack slightly to add fuel. Various grill-top accessories are available; one of the most useful is a rib rack, which holds several racks of ribs vertically. This allows twice as many racks of ribs to cook at one time.

We suggest regular hardwood charcoal briquettes, not the presoaked kind. Chunk wood charcoal (rather than briquette style) is available in many locations. Our experience is that it burns hotter and longer. We prefer chimney-style starters, which need only a page or two of newspaper to ignite charcoal quickly, or electric starters. If you use lighter fluid, be certain to allow the fire to get uniformly hot before cooking, which will ensure that lighter fluid has burned away. Never add fluid to burning coals!

To start a charcoal fire, open vents on bottom of grill and mound about 3 pounds charcoal in center of charcoal grate. Squirt starter fluid all over charcoal, and allow to soak for 1 minute. Light charcoal. Or, use an electric starter or a chimney starter according to directions. When coals are covered with a gray ash, spread them evenly over the charcoal grate, if using the direct-cooking method, or mound them to one or both sides of the charcoal grate, if using the indirect-cooking method.

An indirect fire uses coals mounded against one or both sides of grill, with food positioned on opposite side from coals or between mounds of coals. Some grills have special metal baskets positioned inside to hold charcoal in the correct position for indirect cooking. A drip pan is often positioned below food to prevent grease flare-ups. Indirect cooking is used particularly for long, slow cooking, as for barbecued ribs. A direct fire uses coals positioned directly below the cooking rack. It is employed to quickly grill foods that do not need long, slow cooking, such as hamburgers or fish steaks or fillets. Foods such as ribs are often cooked slowly using the indirect method, then reheated and crisped over a direct fire using medium heat.

Judging how hot a fire is takes practice, but a time-honored method is to hold your hand 5 or 6 inches above the grate and count off seconds–"one thousand one, one thousand two, one thousand three," and so on. If your hand is uncomfortable after 1 or 2 seconds, the fire is hot. If you can count 3 or 4 seconds, the fire is medium. If you can count 5 or 6 seconds, you have a low fire.

Most flavor in grilling comes when food juices drip onto coals, producing smoke. An extra degree of smokiness can be produced by adding hardwood chips to a fire. An aluminum foil pouch folded around chips, with a few holes poked in it, is a handy package to lay directly on coals. Or, use a small disposable aluminum pan. A couple of handfuls of chips are usually enough to get the job done. Some folks think soaking chips in water to cover for 30 minutes makes for more smoke, while others disagree. If there's no water shortage in your area try both methods to find your favorite!

A long-handled spatula and long-handled spring tongs are valuable grilling tools. The spatula helps prevent burns; the spring tongs don't have to be manually opened, which facilitates turning items on a grill rack. Some cooks like to oil the grill rack before adding food, in which case a heavy-duty natural bristle (not nylon) brush reserved for the purpose is handy.

Barbecue–
Ribs and Chicken,
Coleslaw and Corn

SERVES 12

❉ ❉ ❉

BARBECUED PORK BACK RIBS

GRILLED CHICKEN

CONFETTI APPLE SLAW

CREAMY CORN SALAD WITH
FRESH HERBS
(not pictured)

NECTARINE, APRICOT, PLUM,
AND BERRY COBBLER

❉

Suggested wine:
ZINFANDEL

Other beverages:
BEER, ICED TEA, ICED COFFEE

❉

❋ PLANNING AHEAD ❋

- ◉ The morning of the party, make dressing for apple slaw. Make dressing and assemble other ingredients for corn salad; refrigerate separately. Make and bake cobbler. Prepare rub for ribs.

- ◉ 4½ hours in advance, start fire in grill. Prepare ribs. Assemble apple slaw.

- ◉ 4 hours in advance, grill ribs.

- ◉ 3¼ hours in advance, check ribs, adding more briquettes if necessary. Prepare chicken for grilling.

- ◉ 2½ hours in advance, check ribs and briquettes again.

- ◉ 1 hour in advance, remove ribs from grill, add charcoal, and grill chicken. Dress corn salad.

- ◉ Just before serving, remove chicken from grill. Rewarm ribs.

WE LOVE TO entertain outdoors. There is nothing like serving grilled foods and fresh salads on a warm summer night to good friends who are enjoying each other's company and lively conversation. Whether you are at the beach, in the country, or on an apartment deck, this way of entertaining is always a success. If you work all week long, this menu is terrific. With a bit of organizing ahead, you can look forward to a relaxed day of cooking that gives you a break from your hectic schedule. Of course, this menu would be terrific for a Memorial Day, Fourth of July, or a Labor Day party, too.

Our planning strategy has you grilling both ribs and chicken, the ribs first, followed by the chicken. The two salads and the dessert are all done in advance. Your guests will enjoy the sweet aroma of freshly baked cobbler in the kitchen, and the spice and smoke from grilling on the deck. Be ready to serve—they'll want to eat!

This menu can be served buffet or family style, since your guests will want to make choices. For each setting, include a knife, a fork, and a spoon. Have lots of paper napkins for those eating ribs. You'll also need an entrée plate, a wineglass, and perhaps a water glass for each guest. After you clear the entrée, you can serve cobbler in individual bowls. Decide ahead if you want to serve hot coffee. Iced coffee or iced tea would be a welcome beverage on a warm summer afternoon or evening.

Let the evening drift along and enjoy the sunset, and for the neighbors on the other side of the fence who didn't get invited, the wafting smells of barbecue will just have to do.

❋

Barbecued Pork Back Ribs

SERVES 12

THESE RIBS have less fat and connective tissue than spareribs and so need less cooking time. They can successfully be very slow-smoked over indirect heat in a backyard kettle-style grill or baked in a 225°F oven in about three hours. A mix of dry seasonings, called a rub, is worked into the meat before cooking, and the ribs are served with or without a barbecue sauce. Remember, licking your fingers at a barbecue is considered a compliment to the cook!

4 racks pork back ribs (about 1½ pounds each)
1 bottle (about 28 ounces) barbecue sauce (optional)

Rub

¼ cup salt

½ cup granulated sugar

¼ cup ground cumin

2 teaspoons ground cinnamon

3 teaspoons ground thyme

1 teaspoon ground cayenne pepper

¼ cup plus 2 tablespoons mild paprika

2 tablespoons freshly ground black pepper

About 3½ hours before you want to serve the ribs, light a small mound of charcoal briquettes (if using a chimney-style starter, fill two-thirds full) in a large, kettle-style grill with a lid (page 108). Dry meat with a paper towel, and trim any excess fat. To make rub, combine all ingredients in a small bowl. Use your hands to work about one-fourth of rub into top and bottom of each rack of ribs. Set ribs aside on a large platter or baking sheet.

When briquettes are covered in a gray ash, arrange in a flattened mound against one side of grill. Place a handful of hardwood chips such as hickory, oak, maple, or mesquite in a pouch of perforated aluminum foil or in a disposable aluminum pan and set directly on coals. Position cooking grate with a handle over coals to make adding briquettes easier (some grates have openings under handles for adding charcoal without lifting grate). Lay ribs on grate on opposite side of grill from coals, overlapping ribs, or use a rib rack. Place lid on grill, with vents directly over ribs, about one-third open. The goal is to maintain a very low heat level—170°F to 250°F. Long-probe barbecue thermometers can be used to check internal grill temperature.

About every 45 minutes, check coals, adding a few more briquettes to maintain steady, low heat. After about 3 hours, ribs ought to be done and feel tender when tested with a sharp knife. You should be able to twist and pull a bone out of a rack.

Serve ribs accompanied with barbecue sauce, if desired.

Cook's Notes

⤙ Ribs may be set aside for up to two hours while other foods are being grilled, or they can be wrapped in plastic, and refrigerated up to 4 days. Crisp over a medium-hot grill before serving.

⤙ A gas grill can also be used for this recipe. It helps to have a two-burner unit so you can leave one burner on low and one burner off. Lay ribs on cool side. Wood chips can be placed on the lava rocks over the hot burner, unless your grill has a special smoking device.

⤙ To cook ribs in a conventional oven, be sure it has a fairly accurate thermostat—use an oven thermometer to check temperature. Preheat oven to 225°F, place ribs on a roasting rack in a baking pan lined with aluminum foil to ease cleanup, and bake, uncovered, until tender, about 3 hours. Serve with a bottled, smoky-flavored barbecue sauce.

❊
Grilled Chicken

SERVES 12

WE DON'T USE the word *barbecued* in this recipe since it actually refers to very slow-smoked, naturally chewy cuts of meat such as pork back ribs. The chicken is grilled after the ribs are removed from the grill and fuel is added to create a hotter fire. Unadorned grilled chicken can be world-class food on its own, but a little bottled barbecue sauce brushed on during the final minutes of cooking contributes an appealing tangy sweetness. Be sure that the barbecue sauce, which usually contains sugar, is brushed on the chicken near the end of cooking so that the sugar does not burn.

> 2 frying chickens (2½ to 3½ pounds each),
>   cut into individual portions (leg, thigh, wing,
>   half breast)
> Salt and freshly ground pepper, to taste
> 1 bottle (about 28 ounces) barbecue sauce (optional)

Build a direct fire in a large, kettle-style charcoal grill (page 108). Place chicken in a large mixing bowl and season with salt and pepper. When coals are covered in a gray ash, spread them evenly under cooking grate. Place chicken on grill and cover with lid. Lid vents should be open. (If using a gas grill, set heat on medium or low.) Turn chicken every 10 minutes, closing lid vents if fire flares up. Cook chicken until thigh juices run clear rather than rosy when pierced with tip of a small knife, or until an instant-read thermometer inserted in a thigh registers 170°F, about 25 minutes. During final 5 to 10 minutes of cooking, brush barbecue sauce on chicken, if desired.

COOK'S NOTES

~ *If you have already cooked something on the grill over low heat and the fire is still burning, spread coals directly under cooking grate and add about 12 briquettes. When they are covered in a gray ash, begin cooking.*

~ *If you prefer skinless chicken, remove skin from chicken parts before grilling. Brush with 1 tablespoon vegetable or olive oil to moisten meat, then season with salt and pepper.*

~ *To cook chicken in a conventional oven, preheat oven to 375°F and place chicken on rack in a baking pan lined with aluminum foil to ease cleanup. Roast until an instant-read thermometer inserted in a thigh registers 170°F, about 30 minutes.*

※

Confetti Apple Slaw

SERVES 12

Festive and colorful, this slaw combines clean flavors with a bright presentation. The apples are prepared and added before serving to prevent them from turning brown.

Dressing
¾ cup extra-virgin olive oil
3 tablespoons cider vinegar
1 teaspoon dry mustard
1 teaspoon sugar
1 teaspoon celery seed
1 teaspoon salt
Freshly ground pepper, to taste

Salad
1½ pounds green cabbage (about 1 medium head)
1½ pounds red cabbage (about 1 medium head)
1 orange or red bell pepper, seeded, deveined, and chopped
1 small red onion, peeled and minced
½ cup chopped parsley
2 crisp red apples, such as Gala or Macintosh

To make dressing, combine all dressing ingredients in a jar with a tight-fitting lid. Shake well.

To make slaw, remove wilted outer leaves from cabbages and discard. Rinse and dry cabbages, and cut each in half lengthwise. Remove heavy white core. Thinly slice, then chop coarsely. Place chopped cabbage in a large mixing bowl. Add bell pepper, onion, and parsley. Add dressing and toss with vegetables.

Core, peel, and chop apples. Toss with slaw. Transfer to a serving bowl, cover, and set aside at room temperature until serving.

※

Creamy Corn Salad with Fresh Herbs

SERVES 12

AS AN ALTERNATIVE to serving corn on the cob, we created this summer corn salad. When entertaining centers around grilled foods, it is wonderful to have a couple of dishes that do not require any last-minute attention, except, of course, remembering to serve them! What makes this simple salad so remarkable is using freshly shucked corn—substituting frozen corn kernels would make the salad pale in comparison.

Salad
8 ears fresh corn
1 large red bell pepper (about 12 ounces), seeded, deveined, and cut into ¼-inch dice
½ cup minced fresh parsley
2 tablespoons minced fresh chives
3 tablespoons minced fresh tarragon

Dressing
¾ cup mayonnaise
¼ cup buttermilk
1 tablespoon rice wine vinegar
¼ teaspoon sugar
½ teaspoon salt
1 teaspoon freshly ground black pepper

To make salad, fill an 8- to 10-quart stockpot two-thirds full with water, cover, and bring to a boil over high heat. Prepare corn by peeling back green husks and silk. Remove and discard. Cut corn kernels from each cob by standing ear upright on a cutting board. Use a sharp knife to cut downward along cob. Discard cobs and scoop kernels into a medium mixing bowl. When water boils, add corn. Cook for 3 minutes, drain in a colander, rinse under cold water, and let drain completely. In a large mixing bowl, combine corn, bell pepper, and herbs. Set aside.

To make dressing, in a medium mixing bowl, combine mayonnaise, buttermilk, vinegar, sugar, salt, and pepper. Blend well.

Add dressing to salad. Stir well, cover, and refrigerate up to 2 hours before serving. If preparing salad earlier in the day or the night before, refrigerate salad and dressing separately, then combine just before serving.

❄

Nectarine, Apricot, Plum, and Berry Cobbler

SERVES 12

IT IS HARD to imagine anything more wonderful than a cobbler, crisp, or pie at the end of a dinner alfresco. Serve with a little ice cream, frozen yogurt, or whipped cream.

Filling

8 apricots, halved, pitted, and cut into thick wedges

8 nectarines, halved, pitted, and cut into eighths

4 plums, halved, pitted, and cut into thick wedges

1 pint blueberries

1 tablespoon peeled, minced fresh ginger root

⅔ cup packed dark brown sugar

2 tablespoons cornstarch

¼ cup freshly squeezed lemon juice (about 1 lemon)

Biscuits

3½ cups all-purpose flour, plus flour for dusting

½ cup plus 2 tablespoons granulated sugar

1 teaspoon salt

2 teaspoons baking powder

1 teaspoon baking soda

1 stick (4 ounces) unsalted butter, cold

1 teaspoon pure vanilla extract

1¼ cups buttermilk

2 to 3 tablespoons milk

To make filling, in a large mixing bowl, combine apricots, nectarines, plums, blueberries, and ginger root. Gently mix. In a small mixing bowl, blend brown sugar, cornstarch, and lemon juice until sugar and cornstarch are dissolved. Add to reserved fruit and stir gently to blend. Spoon into a 10-by-14-inch glass or ceramic baking dish with sides 2 to 2½ inches high. Set aside.

Preheat oven to 400° F. To make biscuits, in a large bowl, combine flour, ½ cup sugar, salt, baking powder, and baking soda. Cut butter into small cubes and scatter over flour mixture. Working quickly, blend butter into flour with your fingertips or a pastry blender until it is the texture of coarse meal. In a small bowl, combine vanilla and buttermilk. Use a spoon to blend buttermilk mixture into flour and stir until all moisture is absorbed. Turn dough out onto a floured work surface. Dust top of dough with flour, then roll dough into a circle ½ to ¾ inch thick. Cut biscuits with a 3-inch round cookie cutter. Press scraps together and form additional biscuits. You should have 12 to 15 biscuits.

Place biscuits close together over the fruit. Brush biscuits with milk using a pastry brush, then sprinkle with 2 tablespoons sugar. Bake cobbler until biscuits are nicely browned, 30 to 40 minutes. Let cool on a wire rack. Set aside at room temperature until serving.

Cook's Notes

The biscuit dough can be mixed in a food processor fitted with the metal blade or in a mixer with a pastry paddle. Follow the same steps—mix dry ingredients, cut in butter, then add liquid and process just until combined.

The cobbler is best made the day of serving. It can certainly be assembled and baked in the morning, kept at room temperature, and served in the evening.

Seafood and Vegetables on the Grill

SERVES 8

✳ ✳ ✳

SCALLOP, SWEET ONION, AND
PAPAYA KEBOBS
(not pictured)

GRILLED SWORDFISH WITH
MEDITERRANEAN HOT-PEPPER
AND ALMOND SAUCE

COUSCOUS WITH APRICOTS
AND PINE NUTS

GRILLED EGGPLANTS AND ZUCCHINI

CHOCOLATE-BANANA TRIFLE
(not pictured)

✳

Suggested wine:
PINOT BLANC

Other beverages:
SPARKLING WATER,
ICED HERBAL TEAS, COFFEE

- ◎ 1 or 2 days in advance, make trifle.

- ◎ 1 day in advance, make pepper and almond sauce.

- ◎ The morning of the party, assemble kebobs.

- ◎ 1½ hours in advance, chop ingredients for couscous. Cut zucchini and eggplant; brush with oil.

- ◎ 1 hour in advance, make couscous. Start charcoal fire in grill. (For a gas grill, preheat for 15 minutes.)

- ◎ 30 minutes before serving, grill vegetables. Grill kebobs. Grill swordfish.

THERE ARE LOTS of wonderful things about this menu. The flavors, textures, and visual appeal are divine. The kebobs combine large sea scallops with chunks of papaya and pearl onions; once grilled, they are succulent and sweet. As a contrast, we offer grilled swordfish with a pungent, spicy sauce. Couscous is a perfect side dish, harmonizing the flavors with the addition of apricots. We adore grilled zucchini and eggplant. They're easy to prepare and look great on the plate. Your guests will beg for seconds when they taste the Chocolate-Banana Trifle, a perfect dessert for this menu. Elegant, simple food—it sounds good to us.

Whether you eat inside or out, the setup should be simple. Have at each place a knife, a fork, and a spoon. Use paper or cloth napkins, whichever you prefer. Set a wineglass and a water glass. Decide in advance whether you want to serve individual entrée plates, set up a buffet, or pass platters family-style. Any of these choices will work perfectly well. You certainly have the option to serve both or only one of the seafood entrées. If serving both seafood dishes, our choice would be to have a buffet so guests can choose their preference. For buffet or family-style service, you'll need platters for the kebobs, swordfish, and grilled vegetables. Use a small bowl for the pepper and almond sauce and a large serving bowl for the couscous.

A pitcher full of summer flowers would look great on the table, as would a couple of votive candles in simple holders. Beyond that we wouldn't get too elaborate. Let the food, summer breezes, and sheer joy of entertaining at home fill the bill.

❋

Scallop, Sweet Onion, and Papaya Kebobs

SERVES 8

BEAUTIFUL to look at, easy to prepare, these kebobs combine the delicious flavors of sea scallops with warm, sweet caramelized papaya hot off the grill. We recommend large sea scallops for this dish—bay scallops are too small to thread on skewers. We also call for frozen pearl onions because they are far more readily available than fresh, but if you have fresh, by all means use them.

32 large sea scallops (2 to 2½ pounds total)
2 ripe papayas, peeled, seeded, and cut into
 ½-inch cubes
32 frozen pearl onions, defrosted
Vegetable oil, for brushing
Salt and freshly ground pepper, to taste
2 limes, cut into 4 wedges each

You will need a total of 16 metal or wooden skewers, 12-inches long. If they are shorter, use 6 to 8 more. Wooden skewers should be soaked in water for 20 minutes before assembling kebobs.

Build a direct fire in a large, kettle-style charcoal grill (page 108). Place scallops in a colander, rinse under cold running water, and pat dry with paper towels. Thread scallops, papaya cubes, and onions onto skewers in the following order: 1 papaya cube, 1 scallop, 2 onions, 1 scallop, and 1 papaya cube. Place assembled kebobs on a platter. Brush both sides of kebobs with vegetable oil. Sprinkle with salt and pepper to taste.

When fire is hot, place scallops on grill perpendicular to the grill slats. Cover with lid (vents open) and cook for 3 minutes. Turn and cook until brown and done, about 3 minutes longer. Serve 2 skewers per person on warm plates accompanied with a wedge of lime.

Grilled Swordfish with Mediterranean Hot-Pepper and Almond Sauce

SERVES 8

THIS SAUCE is an adaptation of a Spanish sauce called *romesco*. It is wonderful on all manner of fish and seafood, and is great with lamb and chicken. It is also superb for dunking fresh vegetables. You may substitute other fish for the swordfish steaks. We particularly like tuna or shark. The amount of fish given is designed to serve eight in conjunction with Scallop, Sweet Onion, and Papaya Kebobs.

Sauce
½ cup sliced almonds
2 cloves garlic, peeled
1 cup mayonnaise
1 tablespoon sherry wine vinegar
1 tablespoon tomato paste
¼ teaspoon cayenne pepper
1 teaspoon mild paprika
½ teaspoon salt
Freshly ground black pepper, to taste

1½ pounds swordfish steaks, about 1 inch thick
Vegetable oil, for brushing
Salt and freshly ground black pepper, to taste

To make sauce, preheat oven to 325°F. Place sliced almonds on a rimmed baking sheet and bake until brown, about 10 minutes. Place garlic in a food processor fitted with the metal blade and process to mince. Add almonds and process until minced. Add remaining ingredients to workbowl and process until blended. Alternatively, sauce can be made by mincing garlic and almonds with a chef's knife and combining with other ingredients in a small mixing bowl.

Build a direct fire in a kettle-style charcoal grill (page 108). Brush both sides of swordfish steaks with vegetable oil and season with salt and freshly ground black pepper. Place steaks on a platter. When fire is ready, place fish on grill and cover with lid (vents open). Grill until an instant-read thermometer inserted in center of a steak registers 120°F, 3 to 4 minutes on each side. Steaks will be almost opaque throughout, with just small center portion that is translucent.

Divide fish steaks into 8 pieces and serve on warmed plates with a dollop of sauce.

※

Couscous with Apricots and Pine Nuts

SERVES 8

COUSCOUS (pronounced *COOS-coos*) is a tiny, granular pasta made from ground durum semolina. While unfamiliar to many North Americans, it is widely used in North Africa and the Middle East. It makes an appealing alternative to rice or noodle side dishes. Best of all, it is easy to make, since the couscous you are likely to find in the supermarket is a 10-ounce box of the instant variety, which requires precious little cooking.

1 cup pine nuts
4½ cups Chicken Stock (page 46) or 2 cans
   (16 ounces each) low-sodium chicken broth
1 teaspoon ground cinnamon
20 dried apricots, very coarsely chopped
¼ cup extra-virgin olive oil
2 boxes (10 ounces each) quick-cooking couscous
Freshly ground black pepper to taste
Salt (optional)
⅔ cup thinly sliced scallion tops

Preheat oven to 325°F. Place pine nuts on a rimmed baking sheet and bake until lightly colored, about 10 minutes. Watch carefully so that they don't burn. Set aside.

Bring stock or broth to a boil in a 3-quart saucepan over high heat. Add cinnamon, apricots, olive oil, couscous, and pepper to taste. Stir well, cover, and remove from heat. Let stand 5 minutes. Taste for salt and add if desired. Stir in sliced scallions and reserved pine nuts, and serve.

※

Grilled Eggplants and Zucchini

SERVES 8

GRILLING is a real crowd pleaser when used for vegetables. All it takes is a little seasoning and the grill's heat to give these mild vegetables appealing flavors. The coating of olive oil helps create the smokiness that you're after when grilling.

2 medium eggplants (1 to 1¼ pounds each)
6 medium zucchini (about 2 pounds total)
2 large cloves garlic, peeled and minced
1 cup olive oil
Salt and freshly ground black pepper, to taste

Build a direct fire (page 108). Cut eggplant into ¾-inch slices. There is no need to peel them. Cut zucchini diagonally in ¾-inch pieces. In a small mixing bowl, combine garlic and olive oil. Spread vegetable pieces on a large baking sheet or platter. Use a pastry brush to brush oil on both sides of vegetable pieces. When fire is ready, grill vegetables until browned on one side. Season with salt and pepper to taste. Turn the slices, season to taste, and continue grilling until browned on second side. Remove vegetables from grill while they are still slightly crisp, or they may become mushy as they continue to cook. Grill in batches, if necessary, keeping cooked pieces warm on a platter in a preheated 200°F oven until ready to serve.

COOK'S NOTES

➤ *For increased smoky flavor, grill vegetables at the same time as meat, fowl, or fish. Juices dripping onto the fire will produce smoke that adds flavor to vegetables.*

Chocolate-Banana Trifle

SERVES 8 TO 10

A TRIFLE IS A CLASSIC English dessert consisting of layers of pound or sponge cake, fruit, crème anglaise (a vanilla custard sauce), and flavorings. The dessert is traditionally served in a pedestaled, straight-sided glass bowl (in order to see the layers), but any straight-sided serving bowl will work. This trifle is at its best when made one to two days prior to serving.

Crème Anglaise

1 cup whipping cream

1 cup milk

4 large egg yolks

¼ cup granulated sugar

¼ teaspoon salt

2 teaspoons pure vanilla extract

Chocolate Sauce

8 ounces good-quality semisweet or bittersweet
    baking chocolate, chopped (see Cook's Notes)

¾ cup whipping cream

Pinch salt

¼ cup bourbon, Cognac, or orange-flavored
    brandy (optional)

1 frozen pound cake (10¾ ounces), thawed
    (see Cook's Notes)

6 medium, barely ripe bananas

3 ounces good-quality semisweet or bittersweet
    baking chocolate, grated or shaved, for garnish

To prepare crème anglaise, combine whipping cream and milk in a heavy, 2-quart saucepan. Cook over medium heat just until cream and milk come to a boil. Combine egg yolks, sugar, and salt in a small bowl. Add ½ cup of scalded cream mixture to yolks, whisk to combine, then pour into cream mixture in saucepan. Return saucepan to medium heat, and stir frequently until mixture is thickened and heavily coats a spoon, 3 to 5 minutes. Crème anglaise will be done when it registers 160°F on an instant-read thermometer. Remove from heat, stir in vanilla, and let cool.

To prepare chocolate sauce, combine chocolate, cream, and salt in a 2-quart saucepan. Cook over medium heat, stirring frequently, until chocolate is melted. Remove from heat, stir in liquor, if using, and let cool.

To assemble trifle, have ready a 2½- to 3-quart straight-sided glass serving bowl. Cut cake into ¼-inch-thick slices, then cut slices diagonally in half to form wedges. Peel bananas, then cut into ¼-inch-thick slices. Spoon just enough chocolate sauce to cover bottom of bowl, tilting bowl to spread sauce evenly. Place just enough cake wedges to form a single layer over chocolate. Cake should touch sides of bowl so it is visible through glass. Next add a single layer of bananas. Spoon just enough crème anglaise over bananas to cover. Repeat layering, ending with a layer of crème anglaise. Cover and refrigerate for up to 2 days before serving. Garnish trifle with chocolate just before serving.

COOK'S NOTES

There is good chocolate, and then there is great chocolate. Some of our favorites include Valrhona, Callebaut, and Guittard. We suggest you undertake some serious tasting for yourself!

We use Sara Lee frozen all-butter pound cake for this recipe. Thaw overnight in refrigerator.

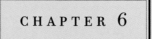

CHAPTER 6

Celebrations and Holidays

✳ ✳ ✳

Celebration Dinner

Thanksgiving

Christmas

New Year's Eve

✳

CELEBRATIONS ARE the punctuation marks and exclamation points in our lives. These are the times when we can slow down and focus on spending time with family and friends, on gatherings. Many of our holidays have their roots in the transitions of the seasons and the abundance that accompanied them. Thanksgiving, of course, is the most obvious. Hence, each year we put forth turkey, cranberry, and pumpkin in some form, as these are the foods always associated with that touchstone of all harvest festivals.

Even though we live in a land of great food abundance, many of us have to watch our diets. So holidays and celebrations give us a welcome excuse to be indulgent for a day. Most cooks feel an overwhelming desire to present a grand spread, but, in the process, feel taxed and overworked. We take your hand and walk you through four wonderful menus for celebrations and holidays. These are the times when planning and organization are essential for successful entertaining. We want you to enjoy and celebrate each holiday along with your guests.

We offer a basic celebration dinner, festive and delicious, that can be used whenever you wish to observe a milestone—birthday, anniversary, graduation, promotion. We have kept to classic themes with our Thanksgiving menu. Christmas dinner is elegant, but not complicated. The New Year's Eve supper focuses on fish and seafood.

Life is a celebration. Use these menus as the exclamation points!

Celebration Dinner

SERVES 6

✳ ✳ ✳

ANCHOVY-GARLIC DIP WITH
BREADSTICKS AND VEGETABLES
(not pictured)

CRACKED PEPPER–GRILLED
DOUBLE-THICK LAMB CHOPS

THE BEST TWICE-BAKED POTATOES

ZUCCHINI AND SCALLION SAUTÉ

COCONUT LAYER CAKE
(not pictured)

✳

Suggested wines:
PINOT GRIGIO WITH DIP,
MERLOT OR CABERNET SAUVIGNON
WITH DINNER

✳

❈ *PLANNING AHEAD* ❈

- ◉ 2 to 3 days in advance, make and refrigerate coconut cake.

- ◉ 1 to 2 days in advance, make and refrigerate anchovy-garlic dip. Prepare and bake potatoes; refrigerate.

- ◉ The morning of the dinner, prepare vegetables for dip and zucchini and scallions for sauté.

- ◉ About 1 hour before serving, marinate lamb chops. Prepare fire for grilling chops. Warm dip.

- ◉ Just before serving, warm potatoes, grill chops, and sauté zucchini and scallions.

Everyone needs a special dinner in their repertoire when the moment requires–for entertaining the boss and his or her spouse, celebrating a special birthday, marking the graduation of a son or daughter from college. This is just such a dinner. It is lovely and elegant, but does not demand great amounts of time in the kitchen. A double-thick lamb chop is a very special piece of meat, but does not require the time or attention of a large roast. Garlic and anchovies are flavors that marry well with lamb; hence the dip becomes a fine start. A special dinner requires a special dessert, and who could resist a beautiful, snowy white coconut cake. It is not too heavy and adds the right element of celebration.

The Anchovy-Garlic Dip is meant to be served as an hors d'oeuvre before dinner. It is best presented in a small pot over a heat source. A little 2-cup saucepan over a candle or small burner works well. If you don't have one, borrow from a friend. Use a platter to arrange the raw vegetables and breadsticks or toasted bread attrac-

tively. It is helpful to provide small plates and plenty of cocktail napkins to prevent drips.

Since this dinner is a celebration, use your best tableware. For each guest, you will need to set out a dessert fork along with a dinner fork, a knife, and a spoon. We strongly recommend cloth napkins for this meal. Fresh flowers and candles always enhance the spirit. Warm the dinner plates before serving. It would be a shame to chill those beautiful chops.

The cake is beautiful to behold. Bring it to the table to cut so all can share in the excitement as you cut the first delicious piece.

Anchovy-Garlic Dip with Breadsticks and Vegetables

SERVES 6

THIS DELICIOUS APPETIZER comes from Italy, where it is called *bagna cauda*. It literally translates as "hot bath," and you may want to take a bath in it when you taste it. Marcella Hazan, the prominent Italian food writer and teacher, refers to this dip as peasant food. Those lucky peasants–garlic, anchovies, butter, and cream, the makings for a great start to a meal. The accompanying vegetables can be prepared hours in advance. Either place in lock-top plastic bags in the refrigerator, or arrange on a serving platter and cover with damp paper towels and refrigerate.

The dip can also be prepared in advance, refrigerated, and then gently warmed. It will look separated, but as it warms, whisk vigorously and it will recombine.

¾ cup extra-virgin olive oil
4 cloves garlic, peeled and thinly sliced
10 anchovy fillets, chopped
½ cup whipping cream
2 tablespoons unsalted butter
Freshly ground pepper, to taste
12 thin, crisp breadsticks or toasted slices of
   French bread
1 red bell pepper, seeded, deveined, and sliced
1 yellow bell pepper, seeded, deveined, and sliced
12 baby carrots
8 ounces small spinach leaves
2 cups broccoli florets
1 dozen scallions with about 2 inches green part

Pour olive oil into a ½-quart saucepan over low heat. Add garlic slices and allow oil and garlic to simmer for 25 minutes. Garlic will brown; be careful it does not burn. Add chopped anchovies to oil, which will make oil sizzle. Stir briefly until anchovies have almost dissolved, about 1 minute. Add whipping cream and cook mixture over low heat until it thickens slightly, about 10 minutes longer. Add butter and a few grinds of pepper.

Place pan over a candle or small burner unit to keep dip warm. Arrange breadsticks or bread and vegetables on a platter. Provide plenty of napkins and small plates to control drips.

Cracked Pepper–Grilled Double-Thick Lamb Chops

SERVES 6

CRACKED PEPPER pressed into lamb chops marinated in Worcestershire sauce before grilling sets the stage for fine eating. Worcestershire sauce is a bottled stew of flavors ranging from vinegar, molasses, and anchovies to tamarind, chili peppers, and shallots. Pretty heady company for a humble lamb chop!

2 tablespoons whole black peppercorns
6 lamb loin or rib chops, 2 inches thick,
   trimmed of visible fat
½ cup Worcestershire sauce

Build a direct fire in a large, kettle-style charcoal grill (page 108). Very coarsely grind peppercorns in a pepper grinder to make cracked pepper. If you don't own a pepper grinder, spread a clean kitchen towel or paper towel on a work surface. Add peppercorns, fold towel over, and force a rolling pin repeatedly back and forth over towel–or pound with a smooth-sided meat pounder or flat bottom of a small, heavy saucepan.

Press ½ teaspoon cracked pepper into each side of each chop. Pour Worcestershire sauce into a 9-by-13-inch baking dish or similar-sized dish. Add chops and marinate at room temperature for 10 minutes. Turn and marinate for 10 minutes longer. Grill over hot coals, turning once, until an instant-read thermometer inserted into center of a chop registers 110°F to 120°F for medium-rare, 5 to 6 minutes per side. Brush with Worcestershire marinade during cooking.

COOK'S NOTES

➤ *Chops can be broiled indoors. Preheat broiler and place ½ inch of water in bottom of broiler pan to control smoke from dripping fat. Broil 4 to 5 inches below heating element or flame and cook to same temperature listed above for grilled medium-rare chops.*

❋
The Best Twice-Baked Potatoes
SERVES 6

WHO DOESN'T LOVE twice-baked potatoes? They combine the creaminess of mashed potatoes with the texture of the potato skin, all in one neat package, making serving simple. They can easily be done a day or two ahead, brought to room temperature, then popped into a hot oven at the last minute.

    6 russet potatoes (about 8 ounces each)
    1 cup whipping cream
    ⅓ cup milk
    1 teaspoon dried tarragon
    1 teaspoon salt
    Freshly ground black pepper, to taste

Preheat oven to 400°F. Scrub potatoes and pierce each one with a fork. Bake directly on center oven rack for 1 hour. Cool potatoes until they can be handled easily, about 10 minutes.

Raise oven temperature to 425°F. Cut each potato in half lengthwise. Use a large spoon to scoop pulp into a medium mixing bowl, being careful not to damage skins. In a 1-quart saucepan over medium-low heat, bring cream and milk to a simmer, then stir into potatoes along with tarragon, salt, and a few grinds of pepper. Use a large, open wire whisk or potato masher to combine all ingredients and whip to a fluffy texture. Taste for seasoning and adjust if desired. Scoop potato mixture back into shells, mounding slightly above skin tops. Place potatoes on a baking sheet large enough to hold them and bake for 10 minutes before serving.

Zucchini and Scallion Sauté

SERVES 6

THIS IS A SIMPLE vegetable accompaniment. The zucchini can be trimmed and cut a few hours in advance and then sautéed shortly before serving. Remember to keep the heat high and your eye on the pan when sautéing.

1½ pounds small, young zucchini (about 6 total)
3 tablespoons extra-virgin olive oil
6 scallions with about 1 inch of green parts, sliced
¼ teaspoon salt
Freshly ground black pepper, to taste
¼ cup chopped fresh parsley, for garnish (optional)

Trim ends of zucchini. Cut each zucchini in half lengthwise and then in half crosswise. Cut each quarter into 5 or 6 sticks, 3 to 4 inches long, depending on size of zucchini.

In a 12-inch sauté pan over medium-high heat, heat olive oil. When hot, add zucchini sticks. Cook, stirring briskly, until beginning to brown at edges, about 4 minutes. Add sliced scallions and continue to cook and stir until scallions begin to soften, about 2 minutes. Add salt and season with a few grinds of pepper. Serve on warm plates, and garnish with chopped parsley, if desired.

Coconut Layer Cake

MAKES ONE 9-INCH CAKE; SERVES 10

THIS CAKE WILL make your mother proud! Your guests will be delighted, and you will be quietly beaming at the thought that you actually produced this beautiful, wonderfully delicious three-layer cake. It can be prepared in stages. This kind of do-ahead preparation makes for really stress-free entertaining.

Sponge Cake
1 tablespoon unsalted butter, softened
2 tablespoons unsalted butter, melted
½ teaspoon pure vanilla extract
1 cup sifted cake flour
2 tablespoons plus ½ cup granulated sugar
4 large eggs
Pinch salt

Filling
¼ cup freshly squeezed orange juice (remove zest from orange first if making optional garnish)
¼ cup dark rum
2 teaspoons granulated sugar
½ cup apricot jam or jelly

Frosting
2½ cups whipping cream
¼ cup granulated sugar
2½ cups plus ½ cup shredded, sweetened coconut (see Cook's Notes)

Garnish (optional)
1 orange
½ cup granulated sugar
¼ cup water

To make cake, preheat oven to 350°F. Prepare a 9-inch round cake pan with 2-inch-high sides. Cut a circle of waxed paper or parchment paper to fit inside bottom of pan. Butter pan using the softened butter, then line bottom with the paper. Combine melted butter and vanilla in a 1-cup glass measure; set aside. Resift flour with 2 tablespoons sugar into a small bowl; set aside.

Place eggs and salt in a large metal or heatproof mixing bowl. Stir to mix. Choose a saucepan or sauté pan that can accommodate mixing bowl with eggs, while holding bowl above bottom 3 inches of pan. Fill pan with water to a depth of 2 inches and bring just to a simmer over medium heat. Add ½ cup sugar to eggs and mix to combine. Set mixing bowl in pan of simmering water; beat and warm egg mixture, using an electric handheld mixer or a whisk, until it is about 3 times the original volume, about 10 minutes. If bowl gets too hot to hold, set on a counter, continue to beat mixture, then return to pan after a minute or so. When mixture is creamy light yellow, and thick enough to write your name, remove bowl from pan, set on counter, and continue beating until cool, about 3 minutes longer.

Sprinkle half of reserved flour mixture over eggs. Using a rubber spatula, gently fold flour into eggs. Rewarm reserved butter mixture if it has solidified, fold into eggs, then fold in remaining flour. Gently pour batter into prepared pan, and bake until sides of cake begin to pull away from pan, about 25 minutes. Cake should rise almost to top of pan and be lightly browned. It should spring back when lightly touched. Set cake on wire rack and let cool completely in pan. Invert cake onto a flat plate or piece of aluminum foil. Tap bottom of pan to unmold cake. Remove waxed or parchment paper, turn cake over so it is right side up, then cover well with plastic wrap and refrigerate at least 2 hours, or up to 3 days, ahead of frosting.

To make filling, combine orange juice, rum, and sugar in a 1-cup glass measure. Stir to dissolve sugar and set aside. Measure apricot jam and set aside.

To make frosting, using an electric mixer or a whisk, whip cream with sugar until it holds soft peaks. Gently fold in 2½ cups coconut. Set aside.

To assemble cake, have ready a long serrated knife and a cake plate. Cut a vertical notch, about ¼ inch deep, in side of cake. This will be your guide for accurately reassembling cake layers. Cut cake horizontally into 3 layers. Don't worry if layers are not perfect–the coconut whipped cream will hide mistakes. Use 4 wide strips of waxed paper or plastic wrap to cover edges of cake plate to protect plate during assembly.

Remove top layer from cake and place cut side up on plate. Using a pastry brush, brush one-third of rum mixture over cake. Spread half of jam over this moistened layer, then spread a very generous 1 cup coconut whipped cream frosting over jam. Place second cake layer on top, lining up the notches. Brush with one-third of rum mixture, and spread with remaining jam and another generous 1 cup of frosting. Place third layer on top, lining up notches. Brush with remaining rum mixture and spread frosting evenly and smoothly over top and sides of cake. Garnish sides and outer edge of top with ½ cup coconut. Slide paper or plastic from plate and clean rim of plate.

Refrigerate cake, loosely wrapped, until ready to serve.

To make optional garnish, use a vegetable peeler or citrus zester to remove zest from orange without cutting into white pith underneath. Try to peel long, wide strips. Use a sharp knife to cut strips into fine matchstick 1½ to 2 inches long. In a small saucepan, combine sugar and water. Stir to dissolve sugar. Bring to a boil over medium-high heat. Add orange zest and simmer 2 minutes. Remove from heat and let zest cool in syrup. When cool, lift zest from syrup, pat dry with paper towels, and arrange attractively around rim of cake. (Zest can be refrigerated in syrup, in a covered jar, for several months. To use, remove from syrup and pat dry on a paper towel.)

Cook's Notes

This cake can also be made with unsweetened coconut chips found in natural-food stores. We like the results and enjoy the texture and flavor.

Here are some strategies for making this cake ahead: Make sponge cake only, freeze for up to 1 month, then thaw overnight in refrigerator, and you are ready to finish the cake. Make sponge cake, refrigerate 2 to 3 days, then layer and frost cake. Make whole cake 2 to 3 days ahead, and refrigerate until ready to serve.

A handheld mixer is the optimal tool for making this cake. If you must use a whisk, we suggest a balloon whisk, but you won't be happy with us unless you plan this to be your substitute for working out at the gym! Ten minutes of whisking eggs, then additional time for whipping cream, demand some motorized assistance.

Parchment paper can in found in well-stocked supermarkets, or in kitchenware shops. It is handy to have on hand for baking.

Thanksgiving

SERVES 12

✳ ✳ ✳

ROSEMARY ROASTED PECANS
(not pictured, recipe page 16)

ROAST TURKEY WITH GIBLET GRAVY

MUSHROOM AND FRESH
HERB STUFFING

PURÉE OF ROAST SWEET POTATOES

CAULIFLOWER AU GRATIN

CRANBERRY CHUTNEY

GREAT PUMPKIN PIE
(not pictured)

✳

Suggested wine:
DRY RIESLING OR PINOT NOIR

✳

❊ PLANNING AHEAD ❊

◉ 1 month in advance, make and refrigerate chutney. Make and freeze roasted pecans.

◉ 1 week in advance, make and freeze pie pastry.

◉ The day before serving, place turkey in brine. Prepare and refrigerate vegetables for stuffing. Make and refrigerate sweet potato purée. Make and refrigerate cauliflower.

◉ The morning of serving, make pie filling and bake pies. Prepare vegetables to roast with turkey. Refresh pecans. Make and bake stuffing.

◉ 2½ hours before serving, roast turkey.

◉ While turkey is resting, make gravy, warm cauliflower and sweet potato purée and stuffing.

THE THANKSGIVING MEAL is one of our biggest food celebrations of the year, filled with tradition and family. We have developed a menu that honors the traditional foods of the holiday in their most delicious forms. We are offering a new, improved method of cooking the turkey. You will never return to Mom's method once you have tasted a brined bird. The bird is accompanied by sweet potatoes, cranberries, and pumpkin, all the flavors that hold Thanksgiving in our hearts.

If your schedule allows, try to get most of the prep done the day before. With this we include setting your table and pulling out serving pieces. Decorating a table can be a lot of fun when you are relaxed. Most likely, this menu will be served buffet style. Plan how and where you are going to place bowls and platters. The Cauliflower Au Gratin can be served directly from its baking dish.

Use a large serving bowl for the sweet potato purée and a smaller bowl for the chutney. Once you have your space arranged, you can decorate with lovely fall flowers and leaves. Colorful gourds spread on the tabletop can add interest as well. If you are seating guests at tables, set out individual place settings. You will need a dinner fork, a dinner knife, a spoon, and a dessert fork at each setting. Also provide water glasses and wineglasses. Cloth napkins are very nice for this holiday. Otherwise, arrange the napkins and silverware attractively at the end of the buffet line so guests won't have to juggle silverware while they are trying to fill their plates.

The day of serving, place two or three bowls of pecans in locations where guests can nibble before dinner.

A whole, brown Thanksgiving bird is a magnificent sight, but impossible to deal with on a buffet. You might want to parade your beautiful bird around to collect the oohs and aahs from your guests and then return to the kitchen to carve it. Place overlapping slices of breast meat on a large platter and surround with wings and legs. Generous sprigs of parsley add color to the platter. If you have a warming tray (or can borrow one), this is a great time to use it to keep the cauliflower and sweet potatoes warm.

We have recommended two wines to accompany this meal. You know your guests–some prefer white and some red. Of course, it's nice to provide both. If you are not setting tables, have a separate area for glasses and wine bottles. Guests can then pour a glass of their favorite once they are through the buffet line.

This menu does require some planning and organization, but the results are well worth it. Follow some simple do-ahead advice and you will have as much fun as your guests. Let's all give thanks for a great meal.

Roast Turkey with Giblet Gravy

SERVES 12 (WITH PLENTY OF LEFTOVERS)

WE ARE GOING to do a sales job here. We want to convince you that, after fifteen years of making Thanksgiving turkey, we have found a method that produces the moistest, most flavorful turkey yet. You see, unlike some of us, turkeys have big breasts. This is a problem, because the white meat typically gets overcooked while the dark meat needs additional roasting. So, we have researched, experimented, and perfected a remarkably easy method to produce a great-tasting bird. The catch, and there is one, is that you have to do some minor preparation twelve to twenty-four hours before roasting your turkey. The work consists of nothing more complicated than marinating the thawed turkey in a brine.

That said, let's talk about the turkey for a moment. Try to buy an organic turkey or, better yet, an organic free-range turkey (one that got to run around and feed in the barnyard instead of being cooped up). At a minimum, buy one that is hormone-free and doesn't have added butter flavor. If the turkey is frozen, it should be defrosted in the refrigerator (never at room temperature) for three to four days.

The last point we want to mention is that we don't believe in stuffing the bird. Blasphemy? We don't think so! For one, it is better in terms of food safety to bake stuffing separately; second, stuffing tastes better when the top is crunchy and crisp.

1 turkey (14 to 16 pounds)

Brine

⅔ cups coarse kosher salt
⅔ cup granulated sugar
5 fresh sage leaves
2 bay leaves
4 sprigs fresh thyme
6 whole cloves
½ teaspoon whole black peppercorns, crushed (see Cook's Notes)
2 teaspoons whole allspice berries, crushed

Spiced Butter

10 whole cloves
2 teaspoons whole black peppercorns, crushed
1 tablespoon whole allspice berries, crushed
1 stick (4 ounces) unsalted butter

Vegetable Mixture

2 large yellow onions (about 1½ pounds total), peeled and diced
2 large carrots (about 8 ounces total), peeled and diced
3 large ribs celery, diced
4 cloves garlic, peeled and minced
7 fresh sage leaves, chopped
1 tablespoon fresh thyme leaves
1 teaspoon salt
Freshly ground black pepper, to taste

Giblet Gravy

2 tablespoons unsalted butter
Neck, tail, and giblets (gizzard, liver, and heart) from turkey
4 cups Chicken Stock (page 46) or 2 cans (16 ounces each) low-sodium chicken broth

2 sprigs fresh thyme
1 bay leaf
6 whole peppercorns
Salt and freshly ground black pepper, to taste
2 tablespoons flour (optional)

To make brine, in a 3- to 4-quart saucepan, combine salt, sugar, sage, bay, thyme, cloves, peppercorns, and allspice. Add 8 cups cold water and stir to combine. Bring to a boil over medium-high heat, continuing to stir to dissolve salt and sugar. Simmer for 3 minutes, remove from heat, add 4 cups cold water, stir, and set aside. Place one plastic oven bag (see Cook's Notes) inside a second to create a double thickness, then place these bags, open wide, in a large roasting pan. Remove thawed turkey from its wrapping. Remove neck and giblets from cavity, cut off tail, and refrigerate until ready to make gravy. Place bird inside the bags. Stand turkey upright while you pour brine over bird. Add just enough additional cold water to cover bird, but allow room to close bags securely with a twist tie. Place breast side down in pan and refrigerate for 12 to 24 hours.

To make spiced butter, place cloves, peppercorns, and allspice in a 1½-quart saucepan and cook over medium-high heat, stirring frequently, until spices are fragrant, 1 to 2 minutes. Add butter and melt completely; set aside.

To prepare vegetable mixture, combine onions, carrots, celery, garlic, sage, thyme, salt, and a few grinds pepper in a medium mixing bowl. Mix well and set aside.

To make giblet gravy, heat butter in a 2½-quart saucepan over medium-high heat. When hot, add reserved turkey neck, tail, and giblets and brown lightly on all sides. Remove liver and set aside. Add stock or broth, thyme, bay leaf, and peppercorns to pan. Bring to a simmer and cook about 40 minutes. Set aside. With a slotted spoon, remove neck, tail, and giblets from stock or broth and allow to cool. Shred meat from neck, and cut liver, heart, and gizzard into small dice, return to stock or broth, and refrigerate. Discard neck bones and tail.

To roast turkey, position an oven rack at lowest level in oven and another rack just above it. This should allow enough clearance for turkey. Preheat oven to 500°F. Remove turkey from brine. Discard bags, brine, and any cured herbs or spices remaining on bird. Rinse turkey under cold water and pat dry with paper towels. Place ½ cup reserved vegetable mixture inside neck cavity, pull skin over to close, and secure with toothpicks. Place 1½ cups vegetable mixture inside chest cavity. Scatter remainder in bottom of roasting pan and add 2 cups water to pan. Set a roasting rack inside roasting pan. Place bird on roasting rack, breast side up. Tie the legs together with kitchen string. Use your fingers to loosen skin of breast meat and separate skin from meat. Tilt bird slightly and pour spiced butter into this pocket. Spread any spices remaining in saucepan on skin of turkey.

Place bird in oven and roast for 30 minutes. Baste turkey and lower oven temperature to 350°F. Continue to roast turkey, basting it every 30 minutes, until an instant-read thermometer registers 165°F when inserted into thickest part of thigh, 1¾ to 2 hours. Transfer bird, breast side up, to a carving board (see Cook's Notes) and let rest for 15 to 30 minutes before carving to let juices set. Use a spoon to remove vegetable mixture from chest cavity and place in roasting pan. While the turkey is resting, you aren't–now is the time to complete the gravy!

To finish gravy, remove reserved stock or broth and giblets from refrigerator and bring to a simmer over high heat. Pass the pan drippings and vegetables from turkey through a strainer into a large measuring cup or gravy strainer. Use back of a spoon to press down on the softened vegetables and work them through strainer. Add them to simmering stock and stir to combine. Skim any fat that comes to surface of pan juices. Add pan juices to simmering gravy. Taste and season with salt and pepper, if desired. If gravy needs to be thickened, place flour in a 1-cup measure, add a small amount of simmering gravy, blend until smooth, then slowly pour into gravy. Simmer 2 minutes, then pour into a warmed bowl or sauceboat to serve.

To carve turkey, untie legs and remove toothpicks. Using a sharp carving knife and fork, cut down between thigh and body until you feel bone. Twist leg/thigh piece a little until you see thigh joint. Now cut through the joint to separate thigh from body. Cut the joint where leg meets thigh. Now you have a leg and thigh ready for a platter. Repeat on other side of bird. To carve breast meat, start at keel bone that runs along top of breast. Angle knife and cut thin slices of breast meat from one side of bird. Lay slices of meat on platter, overlapping them for a nice presentation. Continue until you reach rib cage, then carve other breast. At this point you should have plenty of meat for serving. Cover bird loosely with aluminum foil and pick the carcass later for fine leftovers. If a guest is determined to have a wing, pull back wing until you see joint between wing and body. Cut through joint to separate wing from body, and add to platter. Serve turkey accompanied with sauceboat of gravy, and enjoy your hard work!

✳

Mushroom and Fresh Herb Stuffing

SERVES 12

AS YOU HAVE gathered from our turkey recipe, we don't stuff our bird. So, here is our version of bread stuffing. It's crusty on top, yet moist from the fresh herbs and vegetables. In our neck of the woods, fabulous bakeries have sprung up producing flavorful, crusty bread. Try to buy some interesting bread and cut your own bread cubes. At Thanksgiving, many bakeries sell dry bread cubes made from their breads. You can also use packaged cubes readily available in supermarkets.

1 tablespoon butter, softened

10 cups dry bread cubes

1 stick (4 ounces) unsalted butter

1 large yellow onion (about 10 ounces), peeled and chopped

2 large carrots (about 8 ounces total), peeled and chopped

3 large ribs celery, chopped

1½ pounds fresh mushrooms, wiped or brushed clean, stems trimmed, and quartered

½ cup minced parsley

1 tablespoon fresh thyme leaves

1 tablespoon chopped fresh sage leaves

1 teaspoon salt

Freshly ground black pepper, to taste

3 large eggs, lightly beaten

4 cups Chicken Stock (page 46) or 2 cans (16 ounces each) low-sodium chicken broth

Preheat oven to 350°F. Coat a deep, 9-by-13-inch baking pan with the tablespoon of softened butter. Place bread cubes in a very large mixing bowl. Melt half the stick of butter in a 10-inch frying pan over medium heat. Add onion, carrots, and celery, and sauté, stirring frequently, until vegetables are soft and lightly golden, 5 to 7 minutes. Add this mixture to bread cubes.

Melt remaining butter in same frying pan over medium heat. Add mushrooms and sauté, stirring frequently, until firm and lightly browned, 4 to 5 minutes. Add parsley, thyme, sage, salt, and a few grinds of pepper, and sauté 1 minute longer. Add mushroom mixture to bread cubes, and stir to combine. Add beaten eggs and stock or broth to bread cubes, and mix well. Place stuffing in prepared dish and bake, uncovered, until top is lightly browned and crusty, about 1 hour. If you have room in your oven, bake stuffing while turkey is roasting. If oven space is tight, bake stuffing prior to roasting turkey, then reheat while you are letting turkey rest and carving it.

Cook's Notes

➤ *Instead of using the turkey liver in the gravy, dice it and sauté it with the onions and other vegetables, then add it to the stuffing. However, if you have vegetarians at your holiday table, use the liver with the giblet gravy, and for the stuffing use canned vegetable broth rather than chicken stock.*

Purée of Roast Sweet Potatoes

SERVES 12

You won't find nuts, marshmallows, honey, or syrup in this dish! Sweet potatoes have a subtle sweetness and need only butter and a bit of salt to brighten and balance their flavor. This purée is easiest to make using a food processor and can be prepared a day or two ahead. For a richer purée, you can substitute milk or half-and-half for the water.

6 pounds sweet potatoes

1 stick (4 ounces) unsalted butter, cut in tablespoon pieces

About 3½ cups hot water

1 teaspoon salt

Freshly ground black pepper, to taste

½ cup chopped fresh parsley

Preheat oven to 450°F. Bake sweet potatoes directly on center oven rack until a fork can be inserted in them without resistance, 40 to 70 minutes, depending on size. Cool until you can handle them safely. Cut potatoes crosswise into 2-inch sections, remove peel with a paring knife, and place sections in a food processor fitted with the metal blade. (You will need to process potatoes in batches unless you have the very largest processor.) Add butter and half the water. Process until potatoes are a smooth consistency with few lumps. Add more water as necessary to thin purée to desired consistency. Add salt and a few grinds of pepper. Taste for seasoning. Transfer to a 2-quart serving bowl and garnish with parsley.

✳

Cauliflower au Gratin

SERVES 12

CAULIFLOWER bathed in a light cheese sauce makes a lovely addition to any fall or winter menu. We like our sauce, also known as a Mornay sauce, lightly thickened and just slightly rich. For added texture, top the gratin with 2 tablespoons of dry bread crumbs.

3 pounds cauliflower (2 heads)

Cheese Sauce
½ stick (2 ounces) unsalted butter
⅓ cup all-purpose flour
3 cups Chicken Stock (page 46) or 1½ cans
    (16 ounces each) low-sodium chicken broth
1 cup whipping cream
6 ounces Swiss cheese, preferably imported, grated

½ teaspoon salt
Freshly ground black pepper, to taste

Remove green leaves from heads of cauliflower. Cut out cores and discard. Break cauliflower into florets, making them fairly uniform in size by cutting larger ones in half or quarters. Rinse florets in a colander and drain.

Select a 3-quart or larger saucepan with a tight-fitting lid. fill with 2 inches of water. Set a collapsible steamer rack or other type of steamer rack in pan; water should be below bottom level of rack. Bring water to a boil over medium high heat. Place cauliflower in pan and cover. Steam florets until just tender when pierced with a fork, 20 to 25 minutes. They should be crisp-tender, not raw, but not mushy.

To make cheese sauce, melt butter in a heavy 2-quart saucepan over medium heat. Add flour and cook flour-butter mixture (also called the roux) over medium heat until bubbly and beginning to smell toasty, 3 to 4 minutes. Heat broth or stock and whipping cream in a microwave or in a 2-quart saucepan until mixture simmers. Add whipping cream mixture to flour-butter mixture and stir well. Continue stirring over medium heat until sauce has thickened and just begins to boil. Add just under half of the grated cheese. Stir until cheese has melted. Remove from heat and add salt and a few grinds of pepper.

Preheat oven to 375°F. Place cauliflower in an oven-proof baking dish large enough to hold it in one layer. Cover with cheese sauce and sprinkle with remaining grated cheese. Bake until mixture is bubbly and cheese is beginning to brown, about 20 minutes.

Cranberry Chutney

MAKES ABOUT 2 QUARTS CHUTNEY

THIS CHUTNEY is a favorite because we love the taste, texture, and ease of preparation. We make the chutney up to one month in advance of Thanksgiving, which leaves us one less thing to think about. You can give this chutney as a gift throughout the holiday season–just pack it into attractive glass jars, and tie a ribbon and a gift tag around the neck of the jar. It will impress!

4 cups fresh or frozen whole cranberries, picked
    over, and stems removed (see Cook's Notes)
2½ cups granulated sugar
6 whole cloves
2 cinnamon sticks, each about 3 inches long
½ teaspoon salt
3 Granny Smith apples (about 6 ounces each),
    peeled, cored, and cut into ½-inch dice
3 firm Bosc or Anjou pears (about 6 ounces each),
    peeled, cored, and cut into ½-inch dice
1 small yellow onion (about 4 ounces),
    peeled and diced
1 cup golden raisins
½ cup dried apricots, chopped
½ cup whole hazelnuts, roasted, skins removed,
    and chopped (see Cook's Notes)
2 teaspoons grated lemon zest

In a deep, 6-quart saucepan, combine cranberries, sugar, 1¾ cups water, cloves, cinnamon sticks, and salt. Bring to a boil over medium-high heat, stirring frequently to dissolve sugar. Cook until cranberries pop open, 10 to 12 minutes. Adjust heat so mixture just simmers. Stir in apples, pears, onion, raisins, and apricots. Continue to cook, stirring frequently, until thick, 10 to 15 minutes. Do not overcook, or you'll lose the lovely texture of the fruit. Remove from heat and add hazelnuts and lemon zest. Cool to room temperature. Remove and discard cinnamon sticks and cloves if you can find them. Refrigerate in tightly sealed jars up to 3 months.

COOK'S NOTES

➤ *Fresh cranberries should be firm and bright red. Always look them over and discard any that are shriveled or underripe.*

➤ *Try to buy shelled hazelnuts, with the skins removed. If the skins are on, place nuts on a rimmed baking sheet and roast in a preheated 375°F oven for 20 minutes. Lay them on a clean kitchen towel, or between several sheets of paper towels, and rub nuts to remove most of skins (they never completely come off). You can substitute blanched almonds, if necessary. Buy them already blanched, and roast like hazelnuts, until slightly browned, 15 to 20 minutes.*

Great Pumpkin Pie

MAKES TWO 9- OR 10-INCH PIES; SERVES 16 TO 20

THE TRADITIONAL FOODS of Thanksgiving are fairly sacred to most Americans. One of them is pumpkin pie. There are many versions and variations out there. We offer what we think is a classic. The custard filling is not too heavy and not too light, and has just the right amount of spices. We freeze the pie shells while making the custard to retard shrinkage. Can you wait a whole year to make this pie again?

1 recipe pie dough (page 64), divided into
    2 equal pieces

Filling
3 cups unsweetened pumpkin purée (one and
    a half 15-ounce cans)
6 large eggs
$\frac{2}{3}$ cup unsulphured molasses
$\frac{1}{4}$ cup granulated sugar
1 tablespoon ground ginger
1 tablespoon ground cinnamon
1 teaspoon ground nutmeg
$\frac{1}{2}$ teaspoon ground allspice
Freshly ground black pepper
2 cups sour cream
1 cup whipping cream
2 tablespoons dark rum (optional)

Topping
1 cup whipping cream
2 tablespoons powdered sugar
2 tablespoons dark rum, optional

Preheat oven to 350°F. Roll out the 2 pieces of pie dough to fit two 9- or 10-inch pie pans. (See directions page 65). Place pie crusts in freezer while making custard filling.

To make filling, place all ingredients, including rum if using, in a very large mixing bowl. Mix very well, preferably with an electric mixer, or by hand with a large whisk, until no white streaks are visible, about 5 min-utes. Divide filling between 2 pie shells. Bake until edges of pies are just beginning to puff and center no longer jiggles like liquid when pies are shaken gently, 45 to 55 minutes. Cool completely.

To make topping, just before serving pies, whip cream with powdered sugar and rum, if using. (We pre-fer our cream lightly whipped so it spoons softly over pie slices.) Slice pies into wedges, top with whipped cream, and serve.

Christmas

SERVES 12

❋ ❋ ❋

CHESTNUT SOUP WITH
MUSHROOM GARNISH
(not pictured)

ROAST TENDERLOIN OF BEEF

WINTER VEGETABLES
BRAISED IN RED WINE

BUTTER LETTUCE AND
TANGERINE SALAD
(not pictured)

CRANBERRY, PECAN, AND
CHOCOLATE FRUITCAKE
(not pictured)

❋

Suggested wine:
CABERNET SAUVIGNON
OR CABERNET-MERLOT BLEND

❋

❊ PLANNING AHEAD ❊

◉ 1 to 2 months in advance (but at least 1 week in advance), make and refrigerate fruitcake.

◉ 2 weeks in advance, roast, peel, and freeze chestnuts.

◉ 1 day in advance, make and refrigerate chestnut soup.

◉ The morning of serving, prepare ingredients for salad, and make dressing.

◉ 2 hours before serving, make mushroom garnish for soup. Prepare vegetables for braising.

◉ 1 hour before serving, prepare roast and place in oven. Braise vegetables. Warm soup.

◉ After main course, dress, toss, and serve salad.

CHRISTMAS IS A TIME to shine, and you will shine with this easy yet elegant menu. There is nothing grander for the Christmas feast than a beautiful piece of beef. A tenderloin is perhaps the most elegant piece of meat you can serve, and is also easy to roast and easy to carve. We surround this entrée with the foods of the season. Chestnuts and mushrooms make a silky first-course soup that is very elegant as well. We continue a seasonal theme by accompanying the roast with winter root vegetables that are braised in red wine. Tangerines are at their best around the holidays, and they are a sweet counterpoint to the salad, which follows the main course. We finish the meal with thin slices of a rich and delicious fruitcake. There will be no more fruitcake jokes after your guests taste this one.

You certainly want to bring forth your best china, crystal, and silver for this dinner. Set your table with a salad fork, a dinner fork, a dinner knife, a teaspoon, and a soup spoon, plus a napkin. Water glasses and wineglasses are needed. Some fresh flowers and candles help add Christmas glitter.

This is a sit-down dinner. Warm the soup bowls for the first course. For the main course, the meat and vegetables can be served on the same platter, if you have one large enough, and you can carve the roast at the table. Warm dinner plates before serving. We like to serve salad after the main course as it is refreshing between rich meat and dessert, but it also works well served between soup and main course. Offer thin slices of cold fruitcake to complete a wonderful holiday meal.

Chestnut Soup
with Mushroom Garnish

SERVES 12

ROASTED CHESTNUTS are fabulous. If you have never peeled and eaten a freshly roasted chestnut, or savored the aromas that will fill your home, then make this soup. Although peeling 2 pounds of chestnuts seems tedious, it can be done two weeks in advance of making the soup. The peeled roasted chestnuts can be frozen, then thawed for one hour before using.

2 pounds fresh chestnuts, about 2½ cups peeled
    (see Cook's Notes)
2 large yellow onions (about 14 ounces each),
    peeled and cut into eighths
3 large carrots, peeled and cut into 1-inch chunks
3 tablespoons olive oil
8 cups Chicken Stock (page 46) or 4 cans
    (16 ounces each) low-sodium chicken broth
1 teaspoon salt
Freshly ground black pepper, to taste
1 cup whipping cream

Mushroom Garnish
2 tablespoons unsalted butter
8 ounces fresh mushrooms, such as shiitake,
    wiped or brushed clean, stems trimmed,
    and thinly sliced (see Cook's Notes)
1 teaspoon fresh thyme leaves
3 tablespoons minced fresh parsley

Preheat oven to 400°F. Using a sharp paring knife, make a long slash on flat side of each chestnut, cutting through outer shell and inner brown skin. Place chestnuts on a rimmed baking sheet and roast until tender when pierced with a fork, about 1 hour. Every 15 minutes, sprinkle chestnuts with a little water.

Place onions and carrots in a 9-by-13-inch baking dish. Drizzle with olive oil and toss vegetables so they are thoroughly coated. Roast until tender when pierced with a fork, about 1 hour. Let cool while you peel chestnuts. (For convenience, you can roast chestnuts and vegetables at the same time.)

While chestnuts are quite warm, but cool enough to handle, peel them. Remove outer shell as well as inner brown skin. Discard any chestnuts that look rotted. Set aside chestnuts that are hard to peel and rewarm in a 400°F oven. Or place on paper towel and rewarm in a microwave for 45 seconds on high. Repeat if needed.

Combine chestnuts and roasted vegetables in a medium mixing bowl. Place one-fourth of chestnuts and vegetables in a blender or in a food processor fitted with the metal blade. Add 2 cups of stock or broth. Process until purée is uniformly coarse rather than smooth in texture. Pour into a 4-quart saucepan. Repeat with remaining chestnuts, vegetables, and stock. Add salt and a few grinds of pepper. Heat to a simmer and cook about 20 minutes to meld the flavors. Add cream, stir to combine, and remove from heat. Taste and adjust seasonings by adding more salt or pepper if desired. Keep soup warm while you make mushroom garnish, or cool and refrigerate, covered, 2 to 3 days prior to serving.

To make mushroom garnish, melt butter in a 10-inch frying pan over medium-high heat. Add mushrooms, raise heat to high, and sauté, stirring constantly, for 2 minutes. Add thyme and parsley and sauté until liquid in pan evaporates and mushrooms are lightly browned, 2 minutes longer. Set aside until ready to serve. This garnish can be made up to 2 hours prior to serving. Rewarm just before serving.

Ladle soup into heated bowls, and mound a spoonful of garnish in center of each bowl.

COOK'S NOTES

🍂 *If you prefer not to roast your own chestnuts or if you want to make this Christmas recipe at a different time of year when fresh chestnuts are not available, you can buy peeled chestnuts in cans or bottles, at specialty-food stores. Drain any liquid in which they are packed. You will need 2 to 2½ cups of chestnuts. Prepared chestnuts are boiled rather than roasted, resulting in a bit of flavor loss to this soup.*

🍂 *If you can't find shiitake or other interesting mushrooms, use the brown mushrooms called cremini found in most supermarkets. Use white button mushrooms as a last resort!*

❋
Roast Tenderloin of Beef

SERVES 12

SIMPLY PUT, this is one of the most elegant entrées you can serve your guests. Tenderloin of beef is the same cut from which filet mignon steaks are portioned. It is close to foolproof to cook. If you are very lucky, you will have leftover tenderloin to use in another meal. Life could be much worse!

1 whole tenderloin of beef (5 to 7 pounds untrimmed)
2 tablespoons olive oil
Salt and freshly ground black pepper, to taste

Using a sharp chef's or boning knife, trim tenderloin and remove silverskin as for pork tenderloins (page 76). Or request a butcher to provide you with a "peeled and roast-ready tenderloin of beef, silverskin removed." You don't need it tied, larded, or marinated. You will get a beautiful roast about 15 inches long and about 4 inches thick at one end, tapering toward the other end.

Preheat oven to 400° F. Place rack in middle level of oven. Line a 12-by-16-inch rimmed baking sheet with aluminum foil to make cleanup easier. Place a roasting rack on the baking sheet. Rub oil over all sides of meat. Sprinkle with salt and a few grinds of pepper. Place roast on rack, and tuck small "tail" under so thin end of roast becomes thicker and cooks evenly. Secure with kitchen string.

Place tenderloin in oven and roast until done to your preference—110° F to 120° F for medium rare, 130° F to 140° F for medium, 150° F for medium well. To measure temperature, insert an instant-read thermometer in middle of roast after about 35 minutes of roasting time. Meat may be done in 35 minutes, or may take 45 to 50 minutes, depending on your oven and exact weight of roast.

Let roast rest for 5 to 10 minutes to allow juices to set. Place on a carving board and carve across the grain into ¼- to ½-inch slices, beginning at thin end of tenderloin. The last slice or two usually has a little gristle, which isn't visible before carving. You may prefer to reserve it for another use rather than serve to guests.

Winter Vegetables
Braised in Red Wine

SERVES 12

TURNIPS AND PARSNIPS–strangers to many households–reward the diner with their luscious sweetness, while onions and carrots round out the hearty blend. Browning the vegetables gives them a deep, slightly caramelized flavor that enriches the braising liquid.

2 tablespoons olive oil
3 large cloves garlic, peeled and coarsely chopped
3 large red onions (about 8 ounces each), peeled and cut into 1-inch wedges
4 parsnips, peeled and cut into 1-inch pieces
2 pounds turnips or rutabagas, peeled and cut into 1-inch wedges
8 large carrots, peeled and cut into 1-inch pieces
1 cup dry red wine
2 cups Chicken Stock (page 46) or 1 can (16 ounces) low-sodium chicken broth
2 teaspoons celery seed
1 teaspoon salt
Freshly ground black pepper, to taste

In a heavy, wide nonreactive (see Cook's Note) sauté pan or heavy casserole with a 5-quart or larger capacity, heat oil over medium-high heat. Add garlic and allow it to sizzle for a few seconds. Add onions and sauté, stirring occasionally, until slightly browned, about 5 minutes. Using a slotted spoon, remove to a medium mixing bowl. Add remaining vegetables and cook, stirring occasionally, until lightly browned, about 5 minutes.

Browning vegetables may be easier done in 2 batches, depending on size of pan. Return onions to pan, and add wine, stock or broth, celery seed, salt to taste and a few grinds of pepper. Bring to a boil, reduce heat to simmer, cover, and cook about 10 minutes. Uncover, raise heat to medium, and cook 5 minutes. Taste for seasoning, and add more salt or pepper if desired. Using a slotted spoon, transfer vegetables to a serving bowl and keep warm until serving. Pour pan juices into a sauceboat or small pitcher and serve with the vegetables.

COOK'S NOTES

A nonreactive pan is one made of a material that does not react to acidic ingredients such as wine, vinegar, and lemon juice, which can change the flavor of foods. Use pans clad with stainless steel, enamel, or nonstick coating rather than unlined aluminum or cast-iron pans.

Butter Lettuce
and Tangerine Salad

SERVES 12

ONE OF THE JEWELS of winter fruit is the satsuma tangerine. Satsumas are seedless, easy to peel, sweet, and succulent. Paired with butter lettuce and a citrus vinaigrette, the tangerines make a delightful addition to our Christmas dinner.

10 cups butter lettuce leaves (see Cook's Notes)
1 small fennel bulb (about 10 ounces), tops removed, cored, and cut into matchstick strips (see Cook's Notes)

1 small red bell pepper (about 4 ounces), seeded,
    deveined, and cut into matchstick strips
4 satsuma tangerines

Dressing
½ cup extra-virgin olive oil
⅓ cup freshly squeezed orange juice (1 orange)
2 tablespoons freshly squeezed lemon juice
¾ teaspoon salt
1 teaspoon granulated sugar
Freshly ground black pepper, to taste
2 tablespoons minced fresh parsley

Rinse lettuce leaves and dry well in a salad spinner or
with paper towels. In a large mixing bowl (the bigger the
better, for tossing salad), combine lettuce, fennel, and
bell pepper. Set aside until ready to serve. Peel tangerines and remove any white pith clinging to fruit. Separate into sections and set aside.

To make dressing, in a 2-cup glass measure, combine olive oil, orange juice, lemon juice, salt, sugar, and
a few grinds of pepper. Stir well to combine. Taste and
adjust seasonings, adding more salt and pepper if
desired. Set aside until serving.

To assemble salad, add tangerine sections to bowl of
lettuce. Add parsley to dressing, stir dressing well, and
pour over salad. Toss well and divide among individual
salad plates.

COOK'S NOTES
*We like to keep the butter lettuce as whole leaves for
an attractive presentation. You certainly can tear them
into bite-sized pieces if you prefer. If butter lettuce is
unavailable, use green leaf, red leaf, or a mixture of both.*

*In all cases, be sure lettuce is dried well. The dressing
does not adhere to wet lettuce.*

*If you are unfamiliar with fresh fennel, then you are
in for a taste treat. Fennel is similar in texture to celery
and has a slight anise flavor. It is used raw in salads and
can be braised, roasted, or grilled.*

✳

Cranberry, Pecan,
and Chocolate Fruitcake
MAKES TWO 9-INCH CAKES; SERVES 20 TO 24

ALL RIGHT, you've all heard the theory that there is
only one fruitcake in the world and it is continually
being passed. Everyone loves to hate fruitcake—until
now! Our tasters requested seconds on this fruitcake.
The problem is really very simple—garbage in, garbage
out. If you use old, dried fruit, your fruitcake will taste
old and musty. Use good-quality dried fruit that is still
moist, good butter, fresh pecans, and fine chocolate.
Feel free to vary dried fruits, keeping the total propor-
tion at 3 pounds.

1 pound golden raisins
1 pound dried cranberries
8 ounces dried apricots, cut into 2 or 3 pieces each
4 ounces dried figs, cut into 2 or 3 pieces each
4 ounces candied lemon rind
½ cup bourbon whiskey, plus 1 to 1⅓ cups
    bourbon for brushing cakes
2 sticks (½ pound) unsalted butter, plus butter
    for coating pan

1 cup brown sugar

1 cup granulated sugar

4 large eggs

1 cup all-purpose flour

1 teaspoon baking powder

¼ cup cocoa

½ teaspoon ground cinnamon

¼ teaspoon ground mace

1 cup pecan halves

1 cup chocolate chips

2 ounces semisweet chocolate (optional)

2 ounces white chocolate (optional)

2 tablespoons whipping cream

At least a week before baking, pour ½ cup of bourbon over dried fruits in a large mixing bowl. Cover and allow to marinate at least 1 week, stirring every couple of days.

Preheat oven to 250°F. Butter two 9-inch round cake or springform pans with 1½- to 2-inch sides. Cut aluminum foil or parchment paper to fit bottom of pans. Butter one side of foil or paper and place, buttered side up, in pans.

In a very large mixing bowl, cream butter with an electric mixer until soft. Add both sugars and continue to beat until mixture is soft and fluffy. Add eggs, 1 at a time, beating well after each addition. The mixture may look curdled. Add dry ingredients and stir until blended.

Add pecans and chocolate chips to fruit mixture and toss well. (If bowl is not large enough, divide mixture between 2 bowls.) Pour batter over fruit and nut mixture. It will seem like a small amount compared with fruit and nuts. Toss completely. All fruits, nuts, and chocolate chips should be coated with batter. Turn mix-ture into prepared pans, dividing evenly. Press mixture down firmly with a large spatula or with the back of a large spoon.

Bake cakes for 3½ hours. Remove from oven and allow to cool in pans for 30 minutes. Loosen cakes from sides of pan with a thin-bladed knife. Turn each cake gently onto a cooling rack, then turn over, right side up, onto another wire rack. (Be careful at this point as cakes are fragile.) Cool completely. Brush each cake with bourbon. Wrap tightly in plastic wrap and refrigerate. Brush every 2 or 3 days with more bourbon.

When ready to serve, decorate if desired by melting the semisweet chocolate and white chocolate sepa-rately, with 1 tablespoon whipping cream, either in a heavy-bottom 2 cup saucepan over very low heat, or in a microwave. Drizzle melted chocolates over cakes in a zigzag pattern. You can use all of one type of chocolate on one cake or mix the colors. Cut small slices with a sharp knife and serve, well chilled.

New Year's Eve

SERVES 8

✳ ✳ ✳

MUSSELS STEAMED IN
A CURRY BROTH
(not pictured)

BAKED SALMON WITH
BULGUR STUFFING

BROCCOLI WITH LEMON BUTTER

CRÈME BRÛLÉE
(not pictured)

✳

Suggested wines:
SAUVIGNON BLANC OR PINOT GRIS
WITH MUSSELS,
CHARDONNAY WITH MAIN COURSE,
CHAMPAGNE WITH DESSERT

✳

- ◉ 2 days in advance, make, bake, and refrigerate custard for Crème Brûlée.

- ◉ 1 day in advance, make bulgur stuffing for salmon.

- ◉ The morning of serving, prepare broccoli for steaming.

- ◉ About 1 hour before serving, stuff and bake salmon.

- ◉ 30 to 45 minutes before serving caramelize topping on Crème Brûlée and refrigerate.

- ◉ While salmon bakes, steam and serve mussels.

- ◉ 10 minutes before serving salmon, steam broccoli.

WE OFFER AN ALL-SEAFOOD meal to celebrate New Year's. A glorious fish and seafood meal is used in many countries to mark the New Year. It is a delightful choice, as cooking fish is easy and quick.

Mussels in a light curry broth begin our meal. They are accompanied by crusty bread or crunchy breadsticks. A stuffed, whole salmon follows. Salmon may be the king of all fish. It has enough fat to satisfy the avowed meat eater, and when served whole, as here, it presents a grand picture. A bright green vegetable on the side finishes the entrée plate. Dessert is absolutely luscious–a rich and silky custard with a crispy caramelized topping.

We plan this as a sit-down dinner, so each place setting should be set in advance with a dinner fork, a dinner knife, a teaspoon (for the brûlée), a soup spoon, a tiny seafood fork if available, and a napkin. Water glasses and wineglasses are needed at each setting. A little confetti or glitter sprinkled around the table adds a nice touch, as does a horn at each setting to toot in the New Year.

A big, wide soup bowl is the best choice for serving mussels. Warm bowls before serving. It is also nice to provide one or two empty bowls at each end of the table for guests to discard empty mussel shells. (This makes it easier to get every drop of delicious broth.) We recommend preparing the plates in the kitchen as you portion the salmon. Place stuffing and broccoli on each plate and serve. Dinner plates should also be warmed in a low oven prior to serving.

Celebrate the bounty of the sea as you ring in a fine New Year.

❋

Mussels Steamed in a Curry Broth

SERVES 8

HERE'S AN EASY, elegant first course. Set the table with little forks and soup spoons. This way guests can pull mollusks from their shells, then slurp up the flavorful broth. They won't want to miss a drop! If mussels are unavailable, you can use clams.

3½ pounds mussels, in their shells
2 tablespoons unsalted butter
1 tablespoon curry powder
1 small yellow onion (about 4 ounces), peeled and diced
2 sprigs fresh thyme
¾ cup dry white wine
½ cup bottled clam juice
½ teaspoon salt
Freshly ground black pepper, to taste

1 teaspoon freshly squeezed lemon juice

3 tablespoons minced fresh parsley

1 baguette or crusty breadsticks

To prepare mussels, place in a colander and rinse under cold running water. Discard any that do not close after being rinsed. If a mussel feels heavy, chances are it is filled with sand. Try to pry it open; the sand-filled mussels will open easily. Pull off or trim beards–the thick whiskers from between their shells–with a pair of kitchen shears.

Preheat oven to 400°F. Warm bread in oven for 10 minutes.

In a heavy, 6-quart saucepan or Dutch oven fitted with a lid, melt butter over medium heat. Add curry powder and sauté, stirring constantly, for 2 minutes. Add onion and continue sautéing for 2 minutes longer. Add thyme, wine, clam juice, salt, and a few grinds of pepper. Cover and bring broth to a boil over medium-high heat. Add mussels, cover, and steam until mussels have opened, about 5 minutes. Using a slotted spoon, remove mussels to 8 individual bowls. Add lemon juice and parsley to broth. Taste broth, and adjust the flavors by adding more salt or pepper if desired. Ladle broth over mussels, then serve immediately with bread or breadsticks. Place a couple of empty bowls on the table to hold shells.

COOK's NOTES

To turn this recipe into an easy main course, serve it over linguine. Allowing ¼ pound of pasta per person, this recipe will have enough "sauce" for 4 servings.

Baked Salmon with Bulgur Stuffing

SERVES 8

HERE IS A GUARANTEED way to impress guests. Serve a baked fish stuffed with nutty, aromatic bulgur. This is simple if you don't allow the sight of a whole fish to intimidate you. It is best to order a whole fish a couple of days in advance. If one is not available or all are very large, use 4 pounds of large fillets; begin to check temperature after fifteen minutes in the oven and you cook all the stuffing separately.

Bulgur Stuffing

2 cups Chicken Stock (page 46) or 1 can (16 ounces) low-sodium chicken broth

2 tablespoons olive oil

1 medium yellow onion (8 ounces), peeled and chopped

½ cup pine nuts

1 large red bell pepper (6 to 8 ounces), seeded, deveined, and chopped

2 cups medium- or coarse-grained bulgur

1 teaspoon salt

½ teaspoon freshly ground black pepper

½ cup chopped fresh parsley

1 whole salmon with head and tail (6 to 7 pounds)

Juice of 1 lemon

Butter for coating pan

½ cup dry white wine

4 sprigs fresh parsley, for garnish

To make stuffing, in a 1-quart saucepan over medium heat, bring stock or broth to a simmer. In a 4-quart saucepan over medium heat, warm olive oil. Add onion and pine nuts and sauté, stirring frequently, until onion begins to brown, 8 to 10 minutes. Add bell pepper, and cook until it begins to soften, 2 to 3 minutes longer. Add bulgur and stir to coat with oil. Add simmering broth, salt, and pepper. Bring to a boil. Reduce heat and allow mixture to simmer, uncovered, until all liquid has been absorbed, about 20 minutes. Remove from heat and stir in chopped parsley. Let mixture cool completely.

Preheat oven to 400°F. Rinse salmon inside and out under cold running water. Pat dry with paper towels. Cover a large rimmed baking sheet, about 11-by-17 inches, with aluminum foil. Butter foil. Place whole salmon on foil. If pan is not large enough, remove head and/or tail with a heavy-bladed knife after transferring salmon to a cutting board. Sprinkle inside of fish cavity with lemon juice. Spoon cooled stuffing into cavity, mounding it fully and allowing some to tumble out. Place any remaining stuffing in a buttered baking dish. Pour white wine over fish. Cover both salmon and additional pan of stuffing with buttered aluminum foil.

Bake salmon for 30 minutes. Remove foil from salmon and place dish of additional stuffing in oven. Begin to check temperature of salmon after another 10 minutes. When salmon is done, an instant-read thermometer should register 130°F to 140°F when inserted in the thickest part of fish. We prefer our fish at 130°F, when it is a slightly "custardy" texture near bone. If you prefer your fish firmer, cook longer.

Remove fish from oven and let rest 5 minutes. Remove pan of stuffing from oven. Peel away top skin of salmon. If desired, transfer salmon to a large, heated serving platter. This will require supporting it with 2 large spatulas. Alternatively, serve directly from baking sheet. Garnish platter or sheet with sprigs of parsley.

To serve, split top side of fish down center above backbone. Cut squares from each long half and slide off bone with a spatula. Serve each piece with a generous portion of stuffing. When top half of salmon has been served, remove backbone. Turn bottom half over and peel away skin. Continue to cut into serving squares.

※

Broccoli with Lemon Butter

SERVES 8

THIS MENU NEEDS an easy-to-prepare, yet attractive vegetable to accompany the salmon. We picked broccoli embellished with lemon butter, for its color, crunch, and simplicity.

2½ pounds broccoli spears
4 tablespoons unsalted butter, melted
2 tablespoons freshly squeezed lemon juice
¼ teaspoon salt

Place broccoli in a colander, wash under cold running water, and drain. Cut off stalk 2 to 3 inches below florets and discard. Peel remaining stem down to tender, pale green part with a vegetable peeler. Cut into halves or quarters, depending on size. Set aside until ready to cook. Combine butter, lemon juice, and salt in a 1-cup glass measure and set aside.

Select a 3-quart or larger saucepan with a tight-fitting lid, and fill with 2 inches of water. Set a collapsible steamer rack or other type of steamer rack in pan; water should be below bottom level of rack. About 10 minutes before serving, bring water to a boil over medium-high heat. Reduce heat to medium. About 6 minutes before serving, add broccoli and steam, covered, until tender, 4 to 6 minutes. Transfer to a serving dish or divide among entrée plates. Drizzle with lemon butter.

✳
Crème Brûlée

SERVES 8

C USTARDS of various kinds are favorite desserts nearly the world over. Crème brûlée is a custard sporting a crisp disk of caramelized sugar on top. It has a satisfyingly rich flavor and seductive texture but doesn't leave dinner guests overly full. The custard is best made a day ahead and refrigerated overnight. The sugar topping should be caramelized about thirty minutes before serving, and then the crème brûlée should go back in the refrigerator to keep the caramelized topping crisp.

Nonstick cooking spray
9 large egg yolks
9 tablespoons granulated sugar
2¼ cups whipping cream
1½ teaspoons pure vanilla extract
½ teaspoon freshly grated nutmeg or scant
    ¼ teaspoon packaged ground nutmeg
12 tablespoons dark brown sugar

Preheat oven to 275˚F. Spray eight 4-ounce ramekins (see Cook's Note) with nonstick spray. Have ready two 9-by-13-inch baking dishes.

In a medium mixing bowl, whisk yolks until a bit thickened. Add granulated sugar and whisk until dissolved. Add cream, vanilla, and nutmeg, and whisk to mix well. Divide among ramekins. Set 4 ramekins in each baking dish and set baking dishes on middle rack of oven. Pour warm–not hot–water into baking dishes until water comes about two-thirds of the way up outside of ramekins. Bake, uncovered, until a thin-bladed knife inserted into center of a custard comes out clean, about 1 hour and 15 minutes. Remove baking dishes from oven and allow custards to cool in water bath 10 minutes. Remove ramekins to a wire rack to cool for 30 minutes, then cover and refrigerate overnight or at least 4 hours before serving.

About 30 minutes before serving, preheat broiler and adjust rack so it is 5 to 6 inches from heating element or burner. Arrange custards on a baking sheet and sprinkle brown sugar evenly over tops of custards. Place under broiler and allow heat to melt and caramelize sugar. Wisps of rising smoke indicate sugar is almost caramelized. The process takes only a few seconds. The trick is to caramelize the sugar thoroughly without actually blackening and burning it. When topping is a rich brown color, remove ramekins from broiler, cool a couple of minutes, and refrigerate to firm custard. Serve within 30 to 45 minutes.

COOK'S NOTES
➤ *A ramekin is a small soufflé-shaped dish. We recommend porcelain over stoneware because it is somewhat more heat resistant.*

CHAPTER 7

Mixed-Up Menus

✳

Homestyle American

✳

A Lunch of Fruits and Ham

✳

Elegant Winter Dinner

✳

Dinner with Just One
Other Couple

✳

Speedy Dinner for Kids

✳

✳

Dinner When it Sizzles

✳

Low-Fat and Tasty

✳

Southwest Flair

✳

Diet-Conscious Dinner
for Friends

✳

Middle Eastern Medley

✳

✳

Dessert Buffet

✳

Dinner in No Time

✳

Late Summer Supper

✳

Spring Luncheon

✳

Dinner in an Hour

✳

*Y*ou don't have to feel bound by the menus we created for this book. Here are some "mixed-up menus," which use different combinations of our recipes to give you other possibilities. We invite you to try these menus and use them as a springboard to other, great, inspired combinations. Asterisks indicate foods or recipes not included in the book.

Homestyle American

✳ ✳ ✳

Iceberg Lettuce
with Blue Cheese Dressing · 62

Really Good Meatballs · 36

Purée of Roast Sweet Potatoes · 140

Dan's Apple Pie · 64

✳

A Lunch of Fruits and Ham

✳ ✳ ✳

Thick-Sliced Black Forest Ham with
Apricot-Mustard Chutney · 102

Irish Soda Bread · 48

Confetti Apple Slaw · 115

Nectarine, Apricot, Plum, and
Berry Cobbler · 116

✳

Elegant Winter Dinner

✳ ✳ ✳

Cracked Pepper–Grilled
Double-Thick Lamb Chops · 129

Mushroom Rice Pilaf · 84

Cauliflower au Gratin · 141

Crème Brûlée · 157

✳

Dinner with Just One
Other Couple

✳ ✳ ✳

Smoked Salmon Pâté · 26

Chicken and Corn Chowder · 44

Baguette*

Rugelach · 99

✳

Speedy Dinner for Kids

✳ ✳ ✳

Cheese Quesadillas · 56

Roasted Tomato Salsa · 52

Celery and Carrot Sticks · 53

Monster Chocolate
Chunk Cookies · 57

✳

Dinner When it Sizzles

✳ ✳ ✳

CELERY WITH SPICY ASIAN PEANUT BUTTER · 20

ASIAN NOODLE SALAD · 74

GRILLED EGGPLANT AND ZUCCHINI · 122

CARAMEL ICE-CREAM PIE · 77

✳

Low-Fat and Tasty

✳ ✳ ✳

GRILLED SWORDFISH WITH MEDITERRANEAN
HOT-PEPPER AND ALMOND SAUCE · 121

COUSCOUS WITH APRICOTS AND PINE NUTS · 122

GRILLED ASPARAGUS · 76

FRESH STRAWBERRIES
AND FROZEN YOGURT *

✳

Southwest Flair

✳ ✳ ✳

GREAT CHILI · 55

CREAMY CORN SALAD WITH FRESH HERBS · 115

WARM FLOUR TORTILLAS *

ICE CREAM WITH BANANAS,
RUM, AND CREAM · 71

✳

Diet-Conscious Dinner
for Friends

✳ ✳ ✳

SCALLOP, SWEET ONION, AND PAPAYA KEBOBS · 120

GRILLED BABY RED POTATOES *

GREEN BEANS WITH WALNUT VINAIGRETTE · 82

FRESH FRUIT *

✳

Dessert Buffet

✳ ✳ ✳

CARAMEL ICE CREAM PIE · 77

COCONUT MACAROONS DIPPED IN CHOCOLATE · 38

FRESH APPLE CAKE · 85

CHOCOLATE-BANANA TRIFLE · 123

FRESH STRAWBERRIES
AND OTHER SEASONAL FRUIT *

✳

Dinner in No Time

✳ ✳ ✳

PENNE WITH GARLIC
AND TOASTED BREAD CRUMBS · 81

CHILLED ASPARAGUS SALAD · 104

FRESH FRUIT AND CHEESE PLATTER · 49

✳

Late Summer Supper

✳ ✳ ✳

MEDITERRANEAN TOMATO TARTS · 33

SPINACH SALAD WITH MUSHROOMS
AND SWEET RED PEPPERS · 68

ESPRESSO SHORTBREADS · 29

✳

Spring Luncheon

✳ ✳ ✳

BLUE CHEESE SHORTBREAD · 18

SAUTÉED CHICKEN BREASTS WITH
TARRAGON AND LIME · 69

COUSCOUS WITH APRICOTS AND PINE NUTS · 122

FRESH APPLE CAKE · 85

✳

Middle Eastern Medley

✳ ✳ ✳

GRILLED CHICKEN · 114

CUCUMBER YOGURT DIP WITH PITA TOASTS
AND FRESH VEGETABLES · 34

ZUCCHINI AND SCALLION SAUTÉ · 131

FRESH FRUIT SORBET *

✳

Dinner in an Hour

✳ ✳ ✳

MUSSELS STEAMED IN A CURRY BROTH · 154

BUTTER LETTUCE AND TANGERINE SALAD · 149

FRENCH BREAD *

COFFEE ICE CREAM *

✳

INDEX

Table of Equivalents

US/UK	METRIC
oz = ounce	g = gram
lb = pound	kg = kilogram
in = inch	mm = millimeter
ft = foot	cm = centimeter
tbl = tablespoon	ml = milliliter
fl oz = fluid ounce	l = liter
qt = quart	

Weights

US/UK	METRIC	US/UK	METRIC
1 oz	30 g	10 oz	315 g
2 oz	60 g	12 oz (¾ lb)	375 g
3 oz	90 g	14 oz	440 g
4 oz (¼ lb)	125 g	16 oz (1 lb)	500 g
5 oz (⅓ lb)	155 g	1½ lb	750 g
6 oz	185 g	2 lb	1 kg
7 oz	220 g	3 lb	1.5 kg
8 oz (½ lb)	250 g		

Oven Temperatures

FAHRENHEIT	CELSIUS	GAS
250	120	½
275	140	1
300	150	2
325	160	3
350	180	4
375	190	5
400	200	6
425	220	7
450	230	8
475	240	9
500	260	10

Liquids

US	METRIC	UK
2 tbl	30 ml	1 fl oz
¼ cup	60 ml	2 fl oz
⅓ cup	80 ml	3 fl oz
½ cup	125 ml	4 fl oz
⅔ cup	160 ml	5 fl oz
¾ cup	180 ml	6 fl oz
1 cup	250 ml	8 fl oz
1½ cups	375 ml	12 fl oz
2 cups	500 ml	16 fl oz
4 cups/1 qt	1 l	32 fl oz

Length Measures

⅛ in	3 mm
¼ in	6 mm
½ in	12 mm
1 in	2.5 cm
2 in	5 cm
3 in	7.5 cm
4 in	10 cm
5 in	13 cm
6 in	15 cm
7 in	18 cm
8 in	20 cm
9 in	23 cm
10 in	25 cm
11 in	28 cm
12 in/1 ft	30 cm

The exact equivalents in these tables have been rounded for convenience.